MORE GRILLED
TO PERFECTION
CHRIS KNIGHT
RECIPES FROM *LICENSE TO GRILL*

McArthur & Company
Toronto

First published in Canada in 2007 by
McArthur & Company
322 King St. West, Suite 402
Toronto, Ontario
M5V 1J2
www.mcarthur-co.com

Library and Archives Canada Cataloguing in Publication

Knight, Chris, 1960-
More Grilled to perfection : recipes from licence to grill / Chris Knight.

ISBN 978-1-55278-640-6

1. **Barbecue cookery.** I. **Title.**

TX840.B3K553 2007   641.7'6   C2007-902077-1

Design by *Mad Dog Design Inc.*
Front cover author photo by *Lippman Still Pictures*
Printed in Canada by *Transcontinental*

The publisher would like to acknowledge the financial support of the Government
of Canada through the Book Publishing Industry Development Program (BPIDP)
and the Canada Council for our publishing activities. The publisher further wishes
to acknowledge the financial support of the Ontario Arts Council for our publishing
program.

10 9 8 7 6 5 4 3 2 1

To Kathy Doherty, my friend and colleague.
Thanks for putting up with me.

Contents

Foreword 2

POULTRY 11

PORK 47

BEEF 78

LAMB 109

VEGETABLES AND FRUIT 130

SALADS 170

SAUCES 189

FISH 202

SEAFOOD 217

Index 130

Foreword

Welcome to the second volume of recipes from *License To Grill*, the incredibly popular TV series bringing barbecue happiness to good people the planet over. With 104 episodes under our collective (and bulging) belts, we've pretty much grilled and smoked everything there is and then some. Filmed at a secret location somewhere in North America, *License To Grill* quickly became a huge hit and is now seen around the world. Making TV is sort of playtime for grown-ups and LTG was extra fun because we got to do it outside in the sun and eat great food all day long. Beats working.

I've thanked pretty much everyone there is who worked so hard on the show (and this book) in Volume One, so I'm going to save a tree or two and not do the same again. In case you don't have Volume One, let me just advise you it also contains the secret to eternal youth, blueprints for a perpetual motion machine and Elvis' home phone number (you didn't think he was gone did you?). It's well worth going out and getting (shameless plug).

Thank you for watching our show. Thank you for buying our book. Here then is absolutely everything you need to know about how to barbecue and how to do these recipes well:

1. WHAT IS BARBECUE ANYWAY?

There are two ways to barbecue.

First you've got your "low-and-slow." This is cooking at low temperature, with or without smoke, using indirect heat with the lid down for a long period of time. Indirect heat means that whatever you are cooking is placed on one side of the grill surface with the burner beneath it turned off. The heat from the other burner(s) (and the smoke, if smoking) fills the cavity of the barbecue (because the lid is down) and cooks whatever it is you've got in there without any direct contact with the flames from the burner. Low-and-slow indirect cooking is generally used for cuts of meat that are tougher and fattier, which need a longer cooking time to break down the fibers or connective tissue, melt the fat and become something wonderfully tender and flavorful.

Then you've got your "high-and-fast." This is cooking at higher temperatures using direct heat with the lid up for shorter periods of time. Now, this is where barbecue aficionados from the Southern US start harrumphing and shaking their heads. They're going to tell you that this is not barbecuing. Barbecue is low-and-slow and that's it that's all. Cooking high-and-fast is grilling which is completely different than barbecuing. Whatever. If you're cooking outdoors on some sort of grill set over some sort of flame, you're barbecuing. High-and-fast is generally used for leaner cuts of meat, fish, and most veggies.

That's pretty much it. Everything else is a variation on these two cooking methods.

2. KNOW YOUR Q - EVERY ONE IS DIFFERENT

Call me crazy, but I'm going to guess that most of you buying a barbecue cookbook already have a barbecue. They come in all sizes and shapes and price points. Some have upper racks for warming, some have infrared back burners for super fast heating and cooking. Some have rotisseries, others have charcoal pits. Some have side burners for pots and pans, others have built in beer fridges and stereo systems (swear to God, it's true). Look, what really matters is that you've got some sort of barbecue-type thing in your backyard and it's summertime and you're outside with a cold beverage in your hand and some good tunes playing and later on your friends come over and you eat and drink and have a few laughs.

Here are some of the things your barbecue should have:

A lid. No lid means no smoking or indirect heat which means you have to do without half the barbecue experience

Wheels. Yes, wheels. If you're going to smoke a pork butt for 3 hours and the prevailing winds change you'll want to move the barbecue around so everyone sitting on the patio doesn't have to inhale clouds of smoke

A temperature gauge. How else are you going to know the temperature inside the barbecue when the lid is down?

A grill surface. There's lots of yakking about how big your grill surface should be. Obviously if you're popular and have lots of people over all the time then you want a bigger grill surface for all the burgers you have to cook. Here's what you have to remember for good barbecue: at a minimum, the distance between any two items on your grill should be at least the width of your thumb. Not an exact science I know, particularly when you consider the thumb size of your average Blackberry addict. The size of your grill dictates how many steaks or fillets or whatever you can cook at any one time. Just don't overcrowd, okay?

Two burners good, three burners better. The more burners you have, the more heat control you have. This is important for rotisserie cooking and indirect heat cooking.

3. CHARCOAL VS. GAS

Diehard barbecue aficionados are going to tell you that the only way to go is charcoal. I've spent more hours reading up on the difference in taste, texture, et cetera between charcoal and gas than I care to think about. Here are my thoughts on the subject:

Charcoal is fine if you've got the time. A great steak house in Chicago or a quality barbecue joint in Memphis will use charcoal because they've got the pits going all the time and it's part of their charm and cachet. You don't have time to coax the coals when you get home from a hard day's work and want to fire up some chicken breasts for the kids.

If there is a difference in taste, then most of us can't tell. It's sort of like two wine snobs sitting around arguing about whether a '78 Petrus is better than an '82 Petrus. Just open the friggin' wine and pour me a glass please.

Most of us barbecue using gas. All the recipes in this book are set up for gas cooking. There, that settles it.

4. OIL YOUR GRILL!

Sounds like something simple enough to remember but it's one of the most important steps to good barbecue. We shot 104 episodes of *License to Grill* with an average of 5 recipes per show and now and then even we'd forget to oil the grill. Oiling the grill ensures that whatever you are cooking doesn't stick to the superheated grill surface. Ever try to lift a nicely cooked salmon steak off an unoiled grill? Not pretty. Canola oil works well because it has a relatively high smoking point. Pour some oil on a paper towel and use tongs to wipe the entire grill surface. You can also use a mister or a spray can but stand back and watch for flare ups.

5. COOKING WITH STEAMBOATS

The grilling recipes (that would be high-and-fast) in this book tell you to set your barbecue to a variety of temperatures. How do you tell if the temperature is right? Hold your hand 2 inches above the grill surface and count steamboats: 7 for low, 5 for medium, 3 for medium high, and 1-geez-that-hurts for high.

6. HOW TO MAKE A SMOKE POUCH

Lots of the low-and-slow recipes will call for smoking the food as well. You can buy tubes and the like to put your wood chips in but it's just as easy to make your own pouch out of foil. Please note that you can also buy wood *pellets*. You make the pouch the same way you would with wood chips, but there's no need for soaking. Quantities vary and you should check the instructions on the packaging. Here's what you need to do to make one with wood chips:

Soak about 2 cups (500 ml) of wood chips in water for about an hour. Drain and squeeze out the excess water.

Spread the wet chips on one side of a large piece of foil. Sprinkle about a cup (250 ml) of dry chips over the wet ones and mix them together. The dry chips acts as kindling to get things going and the wet ones give you a longer smoking time.

Loosely fold the foil over like you're closing a book. Crimp the edges of the foil to seal the pouch.

Use a fork to puncture a few holes on the top and bottom of the pouch to let the smoke escape.

One pouch should give you about 45 minutes to an hour of smoke.

7. HOW TO RUB A RUB

A rub is a combination of dry granular ingredients applied to the surface of some foodstuff to impart additional flavor. Usually it's a bunch of different spices, sugar and/or salt and dried herbs. What you want to do is apply enough pressure when you're rubbing to tear little micro-pockets in the flesh so as to insinuate the ingredients into the meat. Use more pressure for something hardy like a pork butt, less for something delicate like a piece of fish.

8. HOW TO MARINATE WITH A MARINADE

A marinade is a combination of wet ingredients in which some foodstuff soaks so as to impart additional flavor to the dish. The best way to marinate is in some sort of sealable plastic bag. It takes up less room in the fridge and ensures the liquid is covering the entire surface of whatever it is you're marinating.

9. ROOM TEMP YOUR FOOD

Let's say you're marinating something or that you've prepared a dish in advance and you stick it in the fridge 'til dinner time. Make sure you remove it from the fridge well in advance of sticking it on the barbecue. You want the internal temperature of your dish to be at room temperature when it hits the grill otherwise you'll throw all the suggested cooking times off. The recipes will tell you how long in advance to take it out of the fridge.

10. USE A NON-REACTIVE BOWL

A "non-reactive bowl" is one that is non-porous, usually made of stainless steel, glass or ceramic. This is particularly important when using a marinade or dish that involves some sort of acid, as in vinegars, lemon or lime juice or tomatoes.

11. COOK ON THE BONE WHENEVER YOU CAN

There's tons of flavor in them there bones. Any professional chef will tell you that cooking something with the bone in will impart way more flavor. A rib steak is a rib-eye with the bone still attached and I think tastes way better. A chicken breast cooked on the bone might not lie as flat on the grill but looks and tastes way better. Keep the skin on too (unless otherwise directed in the recipe) for a double flavor boost. Dinner guests watching their waistlines can always leave the skin on the side of the plate.

12. TENT YOUR MEAT!

So you throw a steak or a piece of chicken or something on the grill to cook. I won't bore you with all the connective tissue hoo-hah but basically your dinner shrinks a bit while it's cooking. Think of that tenderloin like a sponge that gets squeezed. Release your grip on the sponge and it relaxes and returns to its original size. The same sort of thing happens on the grill. Take the tenderloin off the heat and cover it in foil so it relaxes and the juices return to all parts of the meat making for a better dinner experience.

13. YOU GRILL WITH THE LID UP AND YOU SMOKE WITH THE LID DOWN

Smoking with the lid down is pretty obvious, but a few words need to be said about grilling with the lid up. There are some guys out there (and I'm not naming names) who grill with the lid down. Wrong. Closing the lid creates a cavity in which the heat from your burners is contained, just like in your kitchen oven. When you grill you're going high-and-fast, so all the heat you need comes from the burner directly beneath the food. By closing the lid, you start cooking the steak or whatever from all sides which in turn throws off all your cooking times. Leave the lid up unless it's snowing.

14. BUY SOME RIB PLIERS

There is a connective membrane that runs along the back of a rack of ribs you need to remove before marinating otherwise the ribs will bunch up on the grill. Buy a pair of pliers and keep them in the kitchen drawer. You can also use them to remove pin bones from fish fillets.

15. GET TO KNOW A BUTCHER AND A FISHMONGER

This really happened to me the other day. I'm in a big grocery store pushing a shopping cart full of things like canned goods, milk, shaving cream and toilet paper. Suddenly, I get a craving for beef short ribs. I love beef short ribs. So I go the meat section and ask the guy in the white smock and he says: "Sorry dude, our meat comes pre-cut in a box and they've already removed the ribs. We never get them." Seriously, go find someone who sells meat and poultry exclusively for a living. Same for fish and shellfish. Do not buy your salmon from someone who also sells personal hygiene products. At a good butcher and fishmonger the quality and selection will be better, plus they'll be able to give you tips and advice and may do special orders when you want something like a rack of venison or Blue Point oysters.

16. BUY FRESH, BUY LOCAL

The less time it takes for something to get from the farm gate to your plate, the better. Fresh is always best. Plus, when you buy local you're supporting someone from your community and that's always a good thing.

17. DO NOT PEEK

You've gone to all the trouble of marinating the ribs overnight and now you're smoking them on the barbecue. Leave them alone! Do not lift the lid to peek at the food. It's still there, I promise you. No sneaky squirrel came along and snatched them. If you lift the lid you let the smoke out and you lower the temperature inside the barbecue. This is not a good thing. If you have to lift the lid to baste or change the smoke pouch, do it quickly.

18. LEAVE IT ALONE

You're grilling a steak or a piece of chicken. Leave it alone. Resist the urge to move the food around on the grill. Let the barbecue do the work. You'll get nice char marks that way. The only exception is if you get flare ups from dripping fat.

19. READ THE WHOLE RECIPE FROM START TO FINISH. NOW READ IT AGAIN.

Your friends are arriving for dinner in a couple of hours. You've just finished making a killer marinade for tonight's barbecue when you read the line in the recipe that says "and marinate for at least 24 hours." *Read the recipe twice*. Also, when I'm reading a recipe I try to envision myself actually doing the steps – sort of the way an athlete does before the big game – which helps me decide whether it's the sort of dish I'm in the mood to make.

20. BUY YOURSELF SOME DECENT TONGS AND SPATULAS

I hate those barbecue sets with the crappy tongs and the flabby spatulas. Go to a restaurant supply store or a gourmet food store and get real ones that work. They don't need wood paneling to be good.

21. AND RUBBER GLOVES TOO

It's a good idea to have a pair of rubber gloves around for skinning and seeding chili peppers so the natural oils don't come in contact with your skin. Otherwise you're in for a world of pain if you rub your eyes. The gloves are pretty handy when you're peeling beets or pitting cherries to prevent your hands from getting all red from the juices

22. MAKE EXTRA AND EXPERIMENT

When it comes to rubs and sauces and marinades, consider the recipes to be more suggestions than directions. Add more or less garlic, take out the coriander, put in some celery salt, double up on the anchovies or hot peppers. Play with recipes to make a flavor profile that best suits your tastes. And make extra to keep in the fridge for a few days – sauces always taste better when they've mellowed a bit.

23. HAVE FUN

It's barbecue, not brain surgery. It's summertime and it's warm out. Life is good. Have fun.

Poultry

Brick Chicken

Grilled Chicken Breasts with Balsamic & Herbs

Grilled Chicken in a White Wine Tarragon Sauce

Grilled Lemonade Chicken

Grilled Stuffed Chicken Breasts

Spicy Barbecued Chicken Legs

Asian Chicken Thighs with Black Bean Sauce

Brown Ale and Maple-Glazed Chicken Wings

Caribbean Style Chicken with a Peanut Brown Sugar Spiced Rub

Chicken Drumsticks Wrapped in Bacon

Chicken Teriyaki

Coffee & Pepper Rubbed Chicken

Port Marinated Smoked Chicken

Smoked Spicy Turkey

Brined Smoked Turkey

Hickory Smoked Turkey Legs

Lemon Grass Smoked Duck

Marmalade Duck

Peking Style Spit-Roasted Duck

Rotisserie Game Hens

Smoked Raspberry Cornish Hens

BRICK CHICKEN

The weight of the brick on top of the bird reduces the cooking time (the brick also transfers heat…sort of) and the combination of the cilantro and lime juice gives this recipe a *zing* when you pop it in your mouth. Make an extra breast and cut it up for lunch the next day on good bread with garlic mayo and your favorite hot sauce.

Rub

2 tsp ground cumin (10ml)

1 tsp ground coriander (5ml)

1/2 tsp salt (2.5ml)

1/2 tsp freshly ground black pepper (2.5ml)

1/2 tsp cinnamon (2.5ml)

1/4 tsp celery salt (1.25ml)

2 tbsp red chili pepper (30ml) - optional

Directions.

- Combine all of the rub ingredients in a small bowl and mix.

- If using whole chicken breasts, cut in half and trim off excess fat.

- Rinse the chicken under cold water and pat dry (this help makes the skin crispy and cleans off any gunk).

- Pat the rub mixture into both sides of each breast and place them in a glass or ceramic dish. Drizzle with 2 tbsp of olive oil and rub again on both sides.

2 whole skinless, boneless chicken breasts

   (12–16 oz each)

(or 4 half breasts, 6–8 ounces each)

1/4 cup extra virgin olive oil (60ml)

4 cloves garlic, finely chopped

1/2 cup fresh cilantro, chopped (125ml)

1/3 cup fresh lime juice (75ml)

2 bricks wrapped in aluminum foil

- Sprinkle with chopped garlic and cilantro.
- Pour the lime juice and remaining olive oil over top and flip the chicken to ensure even coating.
- Place the chicken in a large plastic sealable bag and leave to marinate in the fridge for 1 to 2 hours.
- Preheat the grill to medium/high heat 400F/200C
- Oil the grill. Have a drink.
- Place the chicken on the grill. Place one foil-wrapped brick on top of each 2 breast halves. Leave the lid up.
- After two minutes, lift the brick and rotate the chicken a quarter turn, but do not flip. Replace the brick and continue to cook for another 2 minutes.
- Flip the chicken, place on an angle, replace the brick on top and continue to cook for another 5 minutes, again rotating the breasts a quarter turn after a few minutes.
- Remove the bird from the grill and tent with foil for 5 minutes before serving.
- NOTE: Don't try to eat the brick!

Serves 4

GRILLED CHICKEN BREAST WITH BALSAMIC & HERBS

Herbes de Provence is a classic combination of basil, lavender, marjoram, rosemary, sage, savory and thyme. Those French know a thing or two about cooking. You can find this combo in most major grocery stores these days. Sprinkle a handful over the flames just before you toss the chicken on the grill for a nice smoky burst of flavor.

4 boneless, skinless chicken breasts
   (8oz/ 240g each)

2 tsp herbes de Provence (10ml)

2 tsp Dijon mustard (10ml)

1 tsp onion powder (5ml)

1 tsp garlic powder (5ml)

1/4 cup olive oil (60ml)

1 tbsp balsamic vinegar (15ml)

Pinch of salt

Pinch of pepper

Directions:

- Place chicken breasts into a sealable plastic bag.

- In a small bowl combine herbes de Provence, Dijon, onion powder, garlic powder, oil and balsamic. Mix to combine evenly. Add the salt and pepper.

- Pour the marinade over the chicken. Seal the bag and shake gently to coat the meat thoroughly. Place in refrigerator to marinate for 20 minutes.

- Preheat barbecue to medium heat.

- Remove chicken from the marinade and pat lightly with paper towel to remove excess moisture. Season with salt.

- Oil the grill and place chicken directly over heat.

- Cook for about 6 minutes per side or when the juices run clear when pierced with a fork in the thickest part of the breast.

- Remove chicken from the heat and cover with foil.

- Let rest 5 minutes before serving.

Serves 4

GRILLED CHICKEN IN A WHITE WINE TARRAGON SAUCE

Tarragon has this crazy almost licorice thing going on that's also got a hit of lemon to it. Amazing. It is a classic pairing with white wine (also fruity) and chicken. What makes this recipe so amazing is how few ingredients there are to get such a big taste. Try it once and it will become part of your weeknight go-to recipe file.

6 chicken breasts on the bone

2 tbsp olive oil (30ml)

Juice of 2 lemons

1 cup white wine (250ml)

2 tbsp tarragon, freshly chopped (30ml)

Sauce

3 tbsp shallots, finely diced (45ml)

1 cup white wine (250ml)

2 tbsp tarragon, freshly chopped (30ml)

4 tbsp cold butter (60ml)

Salt and pepper to taste

Directions:

- Place the chicken breasts in a sealable plastic bag.

- In a bowl mix the olive oil, lemon juice, wine and tarragon. Pour over the chicken and seal the bag. Toss to ensure the chicken is well coated. Place in the fridge to marinate for 2 hours.

- Preheat the grill to medium high heat.

- A half hour prior to cooking time, remove the chicken from the fridge and allow the meat to come to room temperature. Remove the chicken from the marinade and pat it dry. Discard the marinade.

- Oil the grill liberally to help avoid sticking.

- Place the chicken breast-side down on the grill. Leave to cook for about 10 minutes and flip. Continue to cook for another 5 minutes.

- Meanwhile, in a saucepan, sauté the diced shallots until translucent but not browned.

- Add white wine and bring to a boil. Reduce heat, add tarragon and leave to simmer and reduce for 10-15 minutes.

- Strain the sauce into a bowl and discard the discolored tarragon.

- Add the butter one knob at a time and whisk until it is all incorporated.

- Season with salt and pepper and drizzle over finished chicken.

Serves 6

GRILLED LEMONADE CHICKEN

Check out the ingredients. The tart concentrated lemonade paired with the salty soy
and the hot sauce zing gets a bump from the garlic and fresh mint. This recipe calls
for chicken legs which gives you the tastier dark meat and added flavor from cooking
"on the bone."

8 chicken legs, bone in

6oz can frozen lemonade concentrate, thawed

1 tbsp soy sauce (15 ml)

A dash of hot sauce

1 tsp celery salt (5 ml)

2 fresh garlic cloves

1/4 cup fresh mint

Salt to season

Pepper to season

Olive oil to coat

Directions:

- Place chicken legs in a large sealable plastic bag.

- Pour the lemonade concentrate into a medium glass bowl.

- Add soy and hot sauces, celery salt, garlic and mint. Mix. Pour the marinade into the plastic bag, coating the chicken. Reserve some marinade for basting.

- Seal the bag and place in the refrigerator to marinate for 2 1/2 hours.

- Half an hour before cooking, remove the chicken legs from marinade and pat dry with paper towel.

- Season the chicken with salt and pepper, drizzle with oil to prevent sticking.

- Preheat the barbecue to medium-high heat 350F/175C. Oil the grill.

- Place the chicken on the grill bone-side down. Sear the meat, then lower the temperature and grill with the lid up for 15 minutes per side.

- Baste the chicken with reserved marinade during the last 10 minutes of cooking.

- Remove the chicken from the grill and tent with foil for 5 minutes before serving

Serves 8

GRILLED STUFFED CHICKEN BREASTS

You can get away with dried oregano for this one but the basil must be fresh. The combo of roasted garlic, lemon and maple syrup will drive everyone at the table nuts.

4 large, whole, boneless, skin on chicken breasts (each 10oz) (each 280g)

1/4 cup chopped fresh basil (60ml)

1/4 cup chopped fresh oregano (60ml)

1 cup goat cheese, crumbled (250ml)

1 tsp chopped lemon zest (5ml)

1 tbsp pure maple syrup (15ml)

2 tbsp toasted pine nuts (30ml)

1 whole head roasted garlic (see note)

Coarse salt and pepper to taste

3 tsp olive oil (15ml)

Directions:

- In a bowl combine crumbled goat cheese, basil, smashed roasted garlic (see directions below), oregano, zest, syrup, pine nuts and salt and pepper.

- Wash and pat the chicken breasts dry and then cut a pocket lengthwise in each.

- Stuff the mixture into the pocket. Not too much. Secure the opening with toothpicks. Coat the chicken with oil.

- Preheat barbecue to medium low.

- Oil the grill.

Roasted garlic

1 head of garlic

1 sprig of fresh thyme

1/2 tsp cracked black pepper (2.5ml)

1 tsp olive oil (5ml)

- Place chicken skin-side down and grill for about 7 minutes or until the skin is golden brown and crispy. DON'T play with it. Let the grill do its job.

- Flip chicken and continue to cook the other side for 7 minutes. Remove from grill. Cover with foil and allow to rest for 5 minutes.

To roast garlic:

- Preheat barbecue to 300F/150C keeping one side off to prepare for indirect cooking.

- Cut the top of a head of garlic.

- Place the garlic onto a sheet of foil, drizzle with oil and cracked pepper and top with a sprig of thyme. Fold in sides of the foil and make a package ready for the grill.

- Place the garlic on the side of the grill with no heat under it. Close lid and cook for 30 minutes or until soft. Remove from grill to cool.

Serves 4

SPICY BARBECUED CHICKEN LEGS

This one has a bit of an Asian thing going on with the lemon juice, fish sauce, ginger and garlic. Delicious. You can find fish sauce in most major grocery chains these days. If your store doesn't carry it then it's time to change grocers.

6 whole chicken legs (drumsticks with
thigh attached)

Marinade

1/4 cup vegetable oil (62ml)

1/4 cup green onions, finely sliced (62ml)

3 tbsp lemon juice (45ml)

1 tbsp fish sauce (15ml)

1 tbsp sugar (15ml)

2 tsp garlic, minced (10ml)

3 tsp ground ginger (15ml)

1 tbsp hot sauce (15ml)

Directions:

- Combine all marinade ingredients in a non-reactive bowl.

- Place chicken legs in a sealable plastic bag and pour marinade mixture over chicken legs; close bag tight and marinate in refrigerator for 4 hours.

- Preheat barbecue to medium high

- Remove the chicken from the marinade and pat dry.

- Lightly brush the legs with oil and season with salt and pepper.

- Oil the grill and place the chicken skin-side down on grill. Cook until golden brown, about 7 minutes. Flip and season other side and continue cooking for another 7 minutes.

- Tent with foil for 5 minutes before serving

Serves 6

ASIAN CHICKEN THIGHS WITH BLACK BEAN SAUCE

Chicken thighs are probably the most underused cut of the bird. Thighs have nice flavorful dark meat and you get to cook on the bone for extra chicken taste. Any pale ale will do instead of Chinese beer for the dipping sauce.

12 boneless, skinless chicken thighs

Marinade

3 tbsp dry sherry (45ml)

2 tsp soy sauce (10ml)

1 tsp white sugar (5ml)

Black Bean Dipping Sauce

1/2 cup black bean sauce (125ml)

1 tsp grated fresh ginger (5ml)

2 green onions sliced thin

1/4 cup Chinese beer (60ml)

1 tbsp white sugar (15ml)

Directions:

- Mix the marinade ingredients until well combined and pour into a plastic baggie. Add the chicken and refrigerate for 30 minutes.

- Remove from the fridge 15 minutes before grilling.

- Preheat the barbeque to medium high.

- Remove the chicken from marinade and pat dry. Discard the leftover marinade.

- Place the chicken on a well oiled grill.

- Grill the chicken for 4 minutes per side or until cooked through and golden brown.

- Remove from grill and cover with foil for 5 minutes before serving.

- Serve with Black Bean Dipping Sauce.

- To prepare Black Bean Dipping Sauce, mix all sauce ingredients in a small bowl.

Serves 6

BROWN ALE AND MAPLE-GLAZED CHICKEN WINGS

Brown ale has a bit more depth of flavor than the pale kind but not as "thick" as the dark lager. Orange, lime, ginger and cilantro in the marinade give the chicken wings a kick you ain't gonna get in your neighborhood pub.

1 1/2 lbs of chicken wings (675g)

Marinade

1 orange, halved and sliced

1 lime, halved and sliced

3 cloves of garlic, chopped

1/2 knob ginger, chopped

1/2 red onion, halved and sliced

1/2 bunch cilantro, chopped

1/2 bottle brown ale

6 tbsp of vegetable oil (90ml)

1 tbsp hot sauce (15ml)

Directions:

- Make the marinade by combining orange and lime slices, garlic, ginger, onion, cilantro, brown ale, vegetable oil and hot sauce in large non-reactive bowl.

- Pour yourself a beer if you'd like. Hey, it's hot outside.

- Place the chicken wings in a large sealable plastic bag, pour marinade over top and marinate in refrigerator for 6 hours, or up to 24 hours. Remove from fridge 30 minutes before grilling.

Brown Ale Maple Glaze

1/2 bottle brown ale

2 cups orange juice (500ml)

3/4 cup maple syrup (175ml)

3 tbsp hot sauce (45ml)

1 tbsp ginger, chopped (5ml)

2 tbsp lemon juice (30ml)

Celery salt to taste

2 tbsp garlic salt (30ml)

- Make the glaze sauce by combining all ingredients in a non-reactive bowl.

- Preheat the barbecue to high and oil the grill

- Place the chicken wings on the grill and cook for about 5 minutes per side.

- Brush the wings with maple glaze sauce and cook an additional minute on each side. Don't do this too early in the cooking process or you'll get flare ups that will ruin the wings

- Serve with the same beer as in the glaze.

Yield: 1 1/2 lbs of chicken wings (675g)

CARIBBEAN STYLE CHICKEN WITH A PEANUT BROWN SUGAR SPICED RUB

The reason we're using thighs for this recipe instead of the more popular chicken breasts is all about the fat. There isn't enough fat on a breast to keep it moist and juicy through a 50 minute cooking process. Remember fat is good, fat is taste, fat is your friend (in moderation of course).

Spice Rub

1/2 cup finely ground roasted peanuts (125ml)

1/4 cup packed light brown sugar (60ml)

1 tbsp kosher salt (15ml)

2 1/4 tsp cayenne (10.1ml)

1 tsp crumbled bay leaf

1/2 tsp plus a pinch ground cloves (2.5ml)

1/2 tsp plus a pinch ground nutmeg (2.5ml)

1/2 tsp ground cinnamon (2.5ml)

1 tsp dried chilies (5ml)

Salt and pepper to taste

10 chicken thighs, skins on, bone in

1 12-oz bottle dark beer

Directions:

- To make the spice rub, combine the peanuts, brown sugar, salt, cayenne, bay leaf, cloves, nutmeg, cinnamon and chilies in a bowl.

- With a small, sharp knife, score each thigh twice on each side, 1/2-inch deep.

- Place the chicken in a large bowl and add the spice rub and toss to coat evenly.

- Prepare the barbecue for indirect grilling. Preheat the barbecue to 250F/110C.

- Place a drip pan over heat source and pour in beer.

- Place the chicken thighs on the side of the barbecue without direct heat.

- Cook chicken thighs over indirect heat with the lid down for 40 to 50 minutes or until juices run clear and skin is crispy.

- Remove from the grill, tent with foil for 5 minutes, plate and serve.

Serves 5

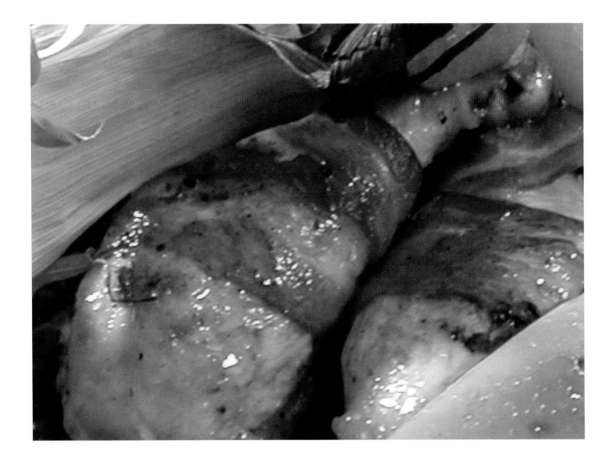

CHICKEN DRUMSTICKS WRAPPED IN BACON

This is *so* easy and *so* good. Look how few instructions there are! Serve these little guys up with a mustard dipping sauce, potato salad and a tall cool drink.

24 chicken drumsticks, washed and dried

2 tsp ground pepper (10ml)

1 lb bacon

1/2 cup olive oil (125ml)

24 toothpicks

Directions:

- Soak toothpicks in cool water for 15 minutes.

- Wrap bacon around the thick part of the chicken, leaving 1-inch at top. Secure bacon with soaked toothpick, season with pepper and drizzle with olive oil.

- Preheat grill to 375F/190C

- Place chicken on grill and cook until bacon is golden brown (7 minutes per side).

Serves 8

26

CHICKEN TERIYAKI

Woo hoo! You get to make your own teriyaki sauce! Once you've done the recipe you can adjust this sauce (and all others in this book) to suit your own personal tastes. For instance, the recipe calls for 1 measly tablespoon of chopped garlic but you can (and should) load up with way more – assuming you don't have a date tonight. Way better than store bought sauce any day plus no shelf stabilizers or artificial preservatives.

1/2 cup soy (125ml)

1/2 cup sherry (125ml)

1/2 cup brown sugar (125ml)

1/4 cup rice wine vinegar (62ml)

1 tbsp garlic, chopped (15ml)

1 1/2 tbsp ginger, grated (22.5ml)

1 tbsp oil (15ml)

8 chicken breasts

bamboo skewers

Directions:

- Add all ingredients (except chicken) to a saucepan and bring to a boil. Reduce heat and simmer for 5 minutes until it thickens and the flavors mingle.

- Let the sauce cool to room temperature.

- Cut the chicken breasts into strips and place in a sealable plastic bag. Pour cooled marinade over top and place in fridge for a minimum of 2 and up to 4 hours.

- Remove the chicken from the fridge 30 minutes before grilling.

- Place the bamboo skewers in water and leave to soak for 30 minutes.

- Thread the chicken strips on the soaked bamboo skewers and place on a tray.

- Preheat the grill to medium high.

- Oil the grill and place the chicken skewers down on the grate on an angle. Rotate halfway after 1 minute to get cross hatch marks.

- Cook for approximately 3 minutes per side or until golden and chicken is cooked through.

Serves 8

COFFEE & PEPPER RUBBED CHICKEN

Coffee and cinnamon give this rub a kick that will have your guests sit up and notice.
The apple slaw is a nice counter-punch to the smoky hot chipotles and lime juice.
This one's a keeper. Use thighs and drumsticks for maximum flavor.

6 chicken thighs with skin and bone in

6 chicken drumsticks

Rub

2 tbsp ground French roast coffee (30ml)

2 tsp freshly ground black pepper (10ml)

1 clove garlic, minced

2 tsp cinnamon (10ml)

1 tsp olive oil (5ml)

2 tbsp brown sugar (30ml)

Salt to taste

Apple Slaw

2 Granny Smith apples, peeled, cored
   and sliced thin

1 chipotle, diced

1 tsp chipotle sauce (5ml)

Juice of 2 limes

1/4 cup red onion, julienned (60ml)

1/4 cup cilantro, chopped (60ml)

Directions:

- In a small bowl, combine rub ingredients. Rub all over chicken.

- Place the chicken in a plastic bag and into the refrigerator overnight.

- Preheat the grill to 350F/180C.

- Place chicken on grill and cook with lid down for 7–8 minutes per side.

- Tent with foil for 5 minutes before serving.

- Serve with Apple Slaw

Apple Slaw Directions:

- Combine all ingredients in a small bowl, cover and refrigerate 1 hour before serving.

Serves 6

PORT MARINATED SMOKED CHICKEN

Port is a fortified wine with a rich deep flavor. You get a wickedly complex yet simple marinade when combined with the rosemary, mustard, garlic and shallots. Try experimenting with different types of wood chips to get the flavors you enjoy the best. In fact, throw extra rosemary twigs right on the flames for a double flavor punch.

Marinade

1/4 cup plus 1 tbsp olive oil (60ml plus 15ml)

1/3 cup ruby port (75ml)

1/4 cup red wine vinegar (60ml)

1/4 cup fresh lemon juice (60ml)

1/4 cup whole grain Dijon mustard (60ml)

3 tbsp rosemary, finely chopped (45ml)

1 tbsp coarsely cracked black pepper (15ml)

1 tbsp garlic salt (15ml)

2 tbsp shallots, minced (30ml)

Directions:

- Rinse the chicken breasts under cold water and pat dry. Place in a sealable plastic bag.

- Combine all of the marinade ingredients (reserving 1 tbsp olive oil) in a non-reactive bowl. Mix together and pour into the bag overtop of the chicken. Seal the bag and place it in the fridge to marinate for 1 hour.

- Place 1 handful of wood chips into water to soak for 30 minutes.

4 chicken breasts, bone in, skin on

Salt and pepper

3 handfuls cherry wood chips

- Prepare the barbecue for indirect cooking by oiling the side the chicken will go on. Crank the other side up to high heat and leave the oiled side turned off.

- Build smoke pouch (see page 5). Place directly over heat source of the grill, close the lid and wait for smoke.

- Drain the chicken from the marinade and scrape off the excess liquid. Rub the chicken with the remaining 1 tbsp of olive oil and season with salt and pepper.

- When smoke starts to billow out, reduce the heat to 200F/100C.

- Quickly lift the lid and place the chicken on the cool side of the barbecue. Close the lid and leave to smoke for 1 hour.

Serves 4

SMOKED SPICY TURKEY

Why do we overlook turkey except at Christmas and Thanksgiving? It's a rich and delicious meat that holds up really well on the barbecue. Any decent butcher would be pleased to sell you the breast alone. In this recipe we get a little mad scientist and inject the meat with flavor. Pickle juice, by the way, is just that: the juice from the jar of pickles in your fridge. You can buy a kitchen syringe at any good kitchen supply or gourmet store. I've even seen them at hardware stores come barbecue season.

Injection liquid

1/3 cup olive oil (83ml)

1/3 cup pickle juice (83ml)

1 tsp yellow mustard (5ml)

2 tsp Worcestershire sauce (10ml)

Directions:

- In a small bowl, mix olive oil, pickle juice, mustard, Worcestershire sauce, and salt and pepper. With a kitchen syringe, pull this mixture up into the syringe and inject it deep into the thickest part of the turkey breast. Repeat this process into different areas and angles of the turkey breast until all of the injection liquid has been used.

5–7 lb turkey breast

Salt and pepper

3 handfuls hickory wood chips

3 handfuls apple wood chips

Hot Times Rub

2 tbsp celery salt (30ml)

2 tbsp brown sugar (30ml)

2 tsp ground cinnamon (10ml)

1 tsp ground clove (5ml)

1/2 tsp dry mustard (2.5ml)

- In a new bowl (like I had to tell you this), combine all of the dry rub ingredients. Massage the rub all over the turkey breast, rubbing it over and under the skin. Place the breast in a sealable plastic bag and refrigerate for 24 hours.

- Remove the turkey from the fridge a half hour before cooking.

- Prepare a smoke pouch (see page 5).

- Prepare the barbecue for smoking over indirect heat by oiling the grill, then firing it up on high heat on one side and no heat on the other.

- Place the smoke pouch directly over high heat source of the grill, close the lid and wait for smoke.

- When smoke begins to billow out of the barbecue, reduce the heat under the smoke pouch to achieve a steady heat of 200F–220F/93C–104C.

- Place the turkey on cool side of the grill and smoke with lid down for 3 1/2 hours. You'll probably have to replace the smoke pouch halfway through.

- Tent with foil for 20 minutes before carving.

Serves 6

BRINED SMOKED TURKEY

Turkeys are big and don't have a whole lot of fat on them, especially the breast meat. So, how do you keep it moist and juicy for an extended cooking time? You brine the bird, baby. Brining means plumping up the meat by soaking it in flavored water. This works well with meats that are lean (no fat means it'll dry out faster) so they remain juicy through a longer cooking process. Try brining before cooking your turkey in your regular oven next Christmas or Thanksgiving – you'll thank me.

WARNING: you're going to cook a whole turkey on a barbecue. This is a challenging recipe. Don't worry, you can do it. It's not difficult, there are just a lot of steps, but trust me – it's worth it. Just make sure you read the ENTIRE recipe three times first. Figure the whole thing out in your head and then go for it.

1 fresh turkey, 12–14 lbs (5.5–6.3 kg)

Brine

2 quarts cranberry juice (2 litres)

2 quarts orange juice (2 litre)

2 small garlic heads, cloves crushed
   but not peeled

1 cup kosher salt (250ml)

4 star anise

1/4 cup coriander seeds (60ml)

1/4 cup whole fennel seeds (60ml)

4 ounces fresh ginger, thinly sliced (120gr)

6 bay leaves

1 tbsp pepper corns (15ml)

2 cinnamon sticks

1 quart water (1 liter)

Rub for turkey

1 tbsp lemon zest (15ml)

1 tbsp cracked pepper (15ml)

2 tsp chilis (10ml)

2 tsp fresh thyme (10ml)

1/2 cup brown sugar (125ml)

2 tsp cinnamon (10ml)

1 tbsp kosher salt (15ml)

To make the brine:

- In a large stockpot, combine the brine ingredients and bring to a boil over high heat until salt dissolves. Remove from the heat. Allow to cool completely.

- Remove the neck and giblets and any excess fat from the turkey and discard. Rinse the bird inside and out, under cold water, drain, and place in the brine and make sure the turkey is completely submerged. Cover and refrigerate for 24 hours.

- Remove turkey from brine an hour before cooking and pat dry with paper towels. Discard the brine.

To make the rub:

- In a bowl, evenly combine lemon zest, cracked pepper, chilis, fresh thyme, brown sugar and cinnamon.

- Rub the mixture vigorously all over the turkey.

- See? That wasn't hard. So far, so good.

Prepare the bird:

- To the cavity of the turkey add lemons, chopped onion, the orange, apple, garlic and thyme.

- Next, truss the turkey and pin the neck skin flap to body using small trussing needles. Place the turkey on a baking sheet.

- Prepare three smoke pouches (see page 5).

Stuffing for turkey

1 whole lemon, cut in half

1 medium sized onion, chopped

1 whole orange, cut in half

1 whole apple, cut in half

1 whole head of garlic, cut in half

6 sprigs of fresh thyme

Drip pan

1 bottle of white wine

Basting Butter

1/2 cup of unsalted butter (125ml)

1/4 cup lemon juice (60ml)

1 tbsp Dijon mustard (15ml)

1/4 cup maple syrup (60ml)

1 tbsp fresh thyme, chopped (15ml)

Salt and pepper to taste

12 cups of hickory wood chips

Make the basting sauce:

- In a skillet over medium heat melt the butter.

- Add lemon juice, Dijon, maple syrup, thyme and salt and pepper. Stir.

Cook the bird:

- Prepare the barbecue for indirect grilling. Preheat the barbecue to high heat. Place the smoke pouch directly over the heat source and a drip pan under the grill on the side that is off. Pour some white wine into the drip pan. Close the lid and wait for smoke.

- Once barbecue is smoking reduce the heat to 220F/110C and place the turkey on the side of the barbecue without direct heat.

- Smoke the turkey over indirect heat for approximately 3–4 hours or until the internal temperature reaches 170F/77C in the breast and 180F/82C
  in the thickest part of the thigh.

- Replace the smoke pouch and add more wine to the drip pan each hour through the cooking time. Baste the bird when you replace the smoke pouch.

- When fully cooked, transfer the turkey to a cutting board or platter, loosely cover the whole bird with foil, and let rest for 40 minutes before carving.

Serves 8

HICKORY SMOKED TURKEY LEGS

I love turkey legs. They have way more flavor than the breast and you get to pull a
Fred Flintstone when you eat them. Sage and thyme are classic go-with herbs for
turkey and the Cajun spice adds an extra flavor boost to the rub. Plus, you get to put
bourbon in this one. No bourbon? No problem. Try using a dark rum or whiskey.

Rub

1 1/2 tsp salt (7.5ml)

1 tsp freshly ground pepper (5ml)

1 tsp fresh sage (5ml)

1 tsp dried thyme (5ml)

1 tsp Cajun spice (5ml)

Grated zest of 1 lemon

4 turkey legs

2 tbsp (30ml) of bourbon

3 handfuls of hickory wood chips

Directions:

- Combine the rub ingredients in small bowl.

- Rinse the turkey legs and pat them dry.

- Apply even amounts of the rub to each leg. Place
  the legs into a sealable plastic bag and refrigerate
  for at least 1 hour up to 6 hours.

- Remove from the fridge 30 minutes before cooking

- Preheat the barbecue to high on one side and oil
  the grill. On the other, leave the heat off.

- Place smoke packages directly over heat source.

- Close the lid and wait for smoke. Reduce heat to
  200F/100C.

- Place the turkey legs on the cool side of the grill
  and close the lid. Smoke for about 2 hours.

Serves 4

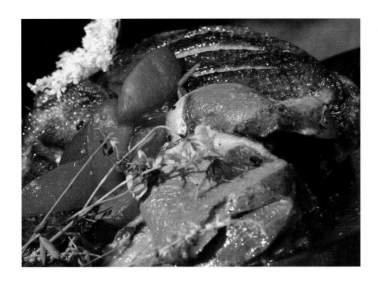

LEMON GRASS SMOKED DUCK

Unlike turkey or chicken breasts, duck has beaucoup fat . . . which is a good thing. We like fat. We love fat. "Fat cap" refers to that nice slab of fat you'll find on top of the breast (or on a cut of beef or pork or anything, including maybe your neighbor). By the way, star anise has a licorice sort-of flavor to it and is a nice counterpoint to the sake in the rub. Sorry, no substitute for sake.

Check out the smoke pouch for this one: black tea, lemon grass, more star anise, raw rice (helps with the smoke) and coriander. Bet you've never done anything like this before, huh?

4 duck breasts, scored fat cap approximately
    9-10 oz each

Rub

1/4 cup sake (60ml)

2 tsp kosher salt (10ml)

1 tbsp fresh minced ginger (15ml)

4 whole dried star anise

1/4 cup vegetable oil (60ml)

2 green onions, coarsely chopped

2 tsp coarsely ground black pepper (10ml)

1 tbsp minced garlic (15ml)

Directions:

- Score fat cap on the duck breast by gently making a diamond pattern in the fat. Ensure you only pierce the fat and not the flesh.

- In a bowl, combine sake, salt, pepper, oil, garlic, green onions and ginger.

- Place the star anise in a coffee grinder and pulse until a light powder is achieved, add to mixture.

- Mix together using a whisk until all ingredients are evenly combined.

- Combine the rub and the duck in a sealable plastic bag and put in the refrigerator to set up overnight.

Smoke pouch

6 tea bags (black tea)

1 whole lemon grass stalk – bashed with
knife and halved lengthwise (this is
done just to release the flavor)

4 cups raw rice (600g)

2 tbsp whole coriander seeds (5ml)

6 whole star anise pods

- Remove duck from refrigerator and take out of the baggie about 30 minutes before cooking.

- Make yourself a smoke pouch (see page 5).

- Prepare the barbecue for indirect grilling. Turn one side on high and leave the other side off. Once you've got some heat going, place the smoke pouch right on the flame and close the lid.

- Once smoke is achieved, turn the heat down to low and let the temperature slip to 220F/110C, then quickly place the duck breast on the side of the barbecue that is off.

- Close the lid and slow-smoke the duck breasts over indirect heat for 50 minutes (note this is for medium rare).

- Remove duck from grill when desired temperature is reached, cover with foil and rest for 10 minutes.

- Slice duck breasts thinly and serve with plum sauce.

Serves 4–6

MARMALADE DUCK

Yes, that's right . . . marmalade. Tangy, tart marmalade with a bit of licorice from the star anise and some heat from the dried chili peppers works amazingly well with the rich duck meat. Cranberry jam or chutney works really well too. Serve the duck with the mango-orange sauce featured along with an arugula salad (arugula is peppery so it'll stand up to the duck) and some grilled sweet potatoes. Two things: PLEASE don't overcook the duck. It ain't no chicken – it's meant to be devoured medium to medium rare. Also, you can remove the remaining fat AFTER the duck is cooked and has sat under foil for 5 minutes. Trust me on this. Wine? Think Zinfandel or Shiraz.

4 whole boneless duck breasts

Marinade

2 star anise

1/2 cup dry white wine (125ml)

1/3 cup orange marmalade (75ml)

1 tbsp canola oil (15ml)

1 garlic clove, minced

1 tsp ground summer savory (5ml)

1/4 tsp of freshly ground pepper (1ml)

1 tsp of dried chili flakes (5ml)

1/4 cup of brown sugar (50ml)

Directions:

- Combine marinade ingredients in a small bowl.

- Put duck into a clear plastic bag and pour in marinade.

- Refrigerate for at least 4 hours and as long as overnight.

- Remove the duck from the marinade and discard plastic bag.

- Score duck skin fat in crisscross pattern with a sharp knife. Ensure you don't cut into duck flesh.

Mango Orange Sauce

1 ripe mango

1/2 cup orange juice (125ml)

1/4 cup liquid honey (50ml)

1 tsp chopped ginger root (5ml)

1 tsp orange peel (5ml)

1/4 tsp salt (1ml)

1/8 tsp white pepper (0.5ml)

- Preheat grill to 350F/180C. You're going to cook with indirect heat here so leave one side off.

- Place duck on oiled grill rack on the side that's turned off. Close the lid and cook for about 10 minutes fat-side up.

- Remove the duck from grill and tent with foil for 5 minutes.

- Fan duck slices on warm plates and garnish with Mango Orange Sauce

Sauce Directions:

- Combine mango, orange juice, honey, ginger root, peel, salt and pepper into a small saucepan. Bring to a boil, reduce heat and cook for about 5 minutes or until fruit is soft.

- Remove from heat and cool slightly.

- Place in a food processor and puree until smooth.

- Return to saucepan to keep warm

Serves 4

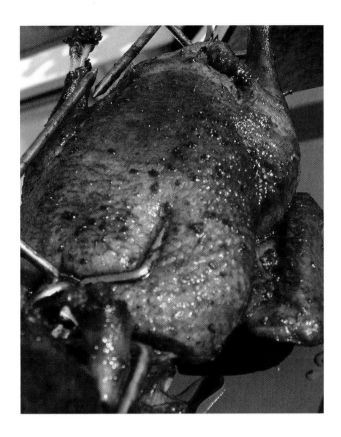

PEKING STYLE SPIT-ROASTED DUCK

There's a lot of fat on a good duck. Slow roasting on a spit will allow the fat to melt off through the meat leaving it moist and juicy with a nice crispy skin.

1 duck, 4 1/2–5lb (2.25–2.5kg)

3 tsp five-spice powder (15ml)

4 tbsp soy sauce (60ml)

3 tbsp sesame oil (45ml)

2 1/2 tbsp rice vinegar (37.5ml)

2 1/2 tbsp fresh ginger, peeled and
*   chopped (37.5ml)*

5 large cloves garlic, finely chopped

3 whole star anise

Sweet-and-sour sauce

Enough water to fill a drip pan halfway

Directions:

- Rinse the duck, inside and out, and pat it dry. Remove and discard any excess fat.

- Using your fingers and starting at the tail cavity, carefully loosen the skin of the duck over the breast and thighs. Rub the five-spice powder under the skin spreading it as evenly as possible.

- In a bowl stir together the soy sauce, sesame oil, vinegar, ginger and garlic. Place the duck in a large sealable plastic bag, pour the marinade in the bag, reserving half for later. Add the star anise.

- Seal bag and refrigerate for at least 4 hours, up to 24 hours.

- Remove the duck from the marinade, pat it dry, then return it to the refrigerator uncovered for 30 minutes to dry the skin further.

- Remove the duck from the refrigerator 30 minutes before grilling.

- Prepare the barbecue for rotisserie roasting over low heat, 200F/100C.

- Truss the duck on the spit according to the manufacturer's instructions.

- Place the water filled drip pan underneath the duck. Depending on your barbecue, the pan might not have enough clearance to fit under the duck, in which case you turn off the heat in the middle, remove the grill and put the pan on the burner.

- Spit-roast the duck, brushing every 1/2 hour with the reserved marinade, until it is a rich golden brown, 1 1/2–2 hours.

- To test for doneness, insert an instant-read thermometer into the thickest part of the thigh away from the bone; it should register 170F/77C. The temperature will rise another 5–10 degrees while the duck is resting under foil for 20 minutes.

- Transfer the duck to a cutting board and slice away. Serve the duck with a warm sweet-and-sour sauce.

Serves 4

ROTISSERIE GAME HENS

You're in for a treat if you've never had a game hen before. This is not white-flesh chicken so be careful not to overcook or you'll end up with something very dry and chewy (that would be a bad thing by the way). You can find them frozen these days in most grocery stores and any decent butcher will either have fresh ones on hand (usually in time for the weekend) or will order you some if you call in advance. You can use dried oregano and sage in a pinch but only fresh rosemary or thyme please. The first gets bitter I find and the second just fades away. Experiment with different mustards in the rub for your own personal touch.

4 game hens about 1 1/2 lbs each, cleaned
   and patted dry

Rub

1 tbsp fresh oregano chopped roughly (15ml)

2 tsp fresh sage chopped roughly (15ml)

1 tbsp fresh rosemary chopped roughly (15ml)

2 tsp fresh thyme chopped fine (10ml)

1 shallot, chopped fine

Directions:

- For the rub: Chop the herbs and mix them in a bowl with the shallots, pepper, Dijon, lemon zest and olive oil.

- Place the cleaned birds in a shallow pan. Rub mixture all over the birds including inside the cavity. Cover with plastic wrap and allow to marinade in the refrigerator overnight.

- Remove the birds from the refrigerator and truss then place them on to a spit, remembering to balance them. Sprinkle all over with kosher salt.

Pepper to taste

1 tbsp Dijon (15ml)

Zest of 2 lemons

1/4 cup olive oil (60ml)

Kosher salt to taste

Drip pan

2 cups of white wine (500ml)

4 sprigs of fresh thyme

- Prepare the barbecue for indirect grilling. Preheat grill to medium high heat.

- Remove center grill and add a drip pan. Add the white wine and fresh thyme to the pan.

- Mount the spit containing the birds to the rotisserie.

- Grill for approximately 40 minutes with the lid up or until skin is golden brown and crispy and juices run clear when pieced with a knife.

- Remove the birds form the barbecue and then from the spit. Tent with foil.

- Let them rest for 10 minutes before plating.

Serves 4–6

SMOKED RASPBERRY CORNISH HENS

Cornish hens are the perfect one-per-person size and these ones are both smoked *and* stuffed. Frozen berries work just as well for a marinade as fresh ones because you don't really care about the consistency. The taste combo of the tart berry, sweet sugar and fresh mint makes for a very interesting marinade.

4 Cornish game hens 1–1 1/2 lbs (500–750 g)

Marinade

1 cup red raspberries (250ml)

1/2 cup rice wine vinegar (125ml)

1 tbsp white sugar (15ml)

Juice of 2 limes

3 cloves garlic, crushed

3 tbsp chopped fresh mint (45ml)

3/4 cup olive oil (190ml)

Salt and pepper to taste

Directions:

- Make 2 smoke pouches.

- Rinse the game hens under cold water and pat dry. By the way, you do this to get rid of gunky stuff and it helps make the skin crispy.

- Combine the marinade ingredients in a medium size non-reactive bowl. Set aside 1/2 cup (125ml) of marinade for basting.

- Place the game hens in 2 large sealable bags. Divide the marinade between the 2 baggies and toss to coat the games hens completely.

Stuffing

2 small white onions

4 stalks of celery

1/2 cup mint leaves (125 ml)

2 lemons sliced thin

Salt and pepper to taste

Butcher twine

6 cups (1250ml) mesquite wood chips

- Place the birds in the refrigerator to marinate for 4 to 6 hours.

- Chop onions and celery into small 1/2-inch (8 mm) pieces. Chop the mint. Slice lemons thin and combine all the stuffing ingredients in a bowl.

- Remove hens from the marinade and pat dry.

- Season the cavity and outside of the bird with salt and pepper.

- Stuff the cavity of the hens loosely with the stuffing. Bind the hens securely with butcher twine.

- Prepare the barbecue for indirect cooking and oil the grill. Preheat to 400F/204C with one side on and the other off. Place the smoke pouch directly over the high heat source and close the lid. Wait for smoke. Once smoke is achieved reduce temperature to 225F/107C or low heat.

- Place hens on cool side of the grill and close lid. The hens will take 1 1/2– 2 hours to cook. Change the smoke pouch halfway through cooking time and baste the hens with reserved raspberry marinade. When hens have 10 minutes cooking time left, baste again. Remove hens from the barbecue and place on a tray.

- Loosely cover with aluminum foil and let rest 10 minutes before serving.

Serves 4

Pork

Two-Way Pork Ribs with Sweet & Tangy Barbecue Sauce
    and Smoky Peach Barbecue Sauce

Beer Smoked Ribs

Dry Jerk Baby Back Ribs

Rotisserie Baby Back Pork Ribs with Balsamic Onion Marmalade

Smoked Ribs with Espresso Barbecue Sauce

Spicy Coconut Ribs

Strawberry & Jalapeno Ribs

Grilled Stuffed Pork Loin

Spicy Jalapeno Stuffed Pork Tenderloin

Pork with Southern Barbecue Sauce

Smoky Canadian Bacon

Smoked Breakfast Bacon

Maple Mustard Pork Burgers

Slow Roasted Pork Butt

Smoked Rotisserie Pig with Root Beet Barbecue Sauce

Hawaiian Piggy on the Cue

TWO-WAY PORK RIBS WITH SWEET & TANGY BARBECUE SAUCE AND SMOKY PEACH BARBECUE SAUCE

There are two kinds of pork ribs and this recipe uses them both. The back ribs are meatier than the spare ribs, but don't have as much fat which means they won't do for longer, slower smoking. In this case you smoke them both at the same time and serve them up with different sauces: tangy barbecue for the spare ribs and smoky peach for the back ribs. Hmmm, you say. Couldn't I just use one or the other? Well, sure. But this way, you get to try them side by side and decide which you like the best. Please, you can thank me later.

Wine? Definitely a spicy Gewürztraminer or fruity Viognier. Beer? Definitely a cold one.

Baby Back Ribs

3 lbs baby back ribs or one side (1.5 kg)

1 tbsp olive oil (15ml)

Salt and pepper to taste

Spare Ribs

3–4 lbs spare ribs (1.5kg) or one side

1 tbsp olive oil (15ml)

Salt and pepper to taste

6 cups hickory wood chips

Smoky Peach Barbecue Sauce

2 cups canned sliced peaches, drained and
their liquid reserved (500ml)

1 cup ketchup (homemade (see page 90)
(250ml)

1/4 cup brown sugar, packed (60ml)

3 tbsp fresh lemon juice (45ml)

1 tbsp peach schnapps (15ml)

1 tsp fresh chopped ginger (5ml)

1 tsp salt (5ml)

1 tsp grated lemon zest (5ml)

pinch of freshly grated nutmeg

1 tsp ground cinnamon (5ml)

1/2 tsp ground allspice (2.5ml)

Directions:

- Use a set of pliers (designated for kitchen) to remove the membrane along the back of ribs. Drizzle the ribs with oil, salt and pepper.

- Prepare 2 smoke pouches *(see page 5)*.

- Prepare the barbecue for indirect grilling. Crank the heat up on one side and add the smoke pouch, close the lid. Once you get smoke, reduce heat to 220F/110C.

- Place ribs on side of the barbecue without direct heat. Smoke the ribs over indirect heat for 3 hours, replacing the smoke pouch halfway through.

- When you change the smoke pouch, baste the ribs liberally with the sauces – tangy barbecue on the back ribs; smoky peach on the spare ribs.

- Close the lid and pour yourself a drink. Go watch the game. Seriously, you must be exhausted. Take a load off.

- Cook for a further hour. Baste again with the sauce and cook for another half hour.

- Once ribs are tender and when gently pulled fall off the bone, remove from grill and tent with foil.

- Serve with extra sauce for dipping and lots of paper towels for chin wiping.

Smoky Peach Barbecue Sauce Directions:

- In a blender combine all ingredients, blend well and pour in to a skillet. Simmer mixture for about 30 minutes, stirring occasionally to avoid scorching the sauce at the bottom of the pan. Remove sauce from heat and serve with pork ribs.

Sweet and Tangy Barbecue Sauce

2 tbsp butter (30ml)

1 small onion, minced

2 cups ketchup (homemade, see recipe on page 90) (500ml)

1/4 cup water (60ml)

1/4 cup apple sauce (60ml)

1/4 cup cider vinegar (60ml)

1/4 cup Worcestershire sauce (60ml)

2 tbsp brown sugar (30ml)

2 tbsp molasses (30ml)

2 tbsp clover honey (30ml)

2 tsp dry mustard powder (10ml)

1 tsp chili seasoning (5ml)

1 tsp garlic powder (5ml)

1 tsp cayenne (5ml)

1 tsp lemon juice (5ml)

1/4 cup bourbon (60 ml)

Sweet and Tangy Barbecue Sauce Directions:

- In a large skillet melt some butter and sauté the onions until they are translucent, about 3 minutes. Add remaining ingredients. Stir to blend ingredients well, and bring to a boil. Reduce heat and simmer for 30 minutes, stirring occasionally to avoid scorching the sauce at the bottom of the pan. Remove sauce from heat and serve with pork ribs.

Serves 6–8 people

BEER SMOKED RIBS

I think guys like to barbecue because you don't really have to do anything. Dump a bunch of stuff in a baggie and leave it in the fridge overnight. Take the stuff out of the bag and put it on the barbecue and leave it alone some more until it's ready. Easy. Plus, this recipe has beer in it!

6 lbs pork spare ribs, or 2 side ribs (2.7 kg)

Marinade

2 (12oz) bottles lager (680ml)
   (One for drip-pan)
3 tbsp lemon juice (45ml)
2 crumbled bay leaf
3 cloves garlic, minced
2 tsp ground cumin (10ml)
2 tsp onion powder (10ml)
2 tbsp chili powder (30ml)
1/4 cup olive oil (60ml)
2 tsp cracked black pepper (10ml)
2 tsp kosher salt (10ml)

6 cups of mesquite wood chips (1.5litre)

Directions:

- Pull the membrane off the back of the ribs using pliers dedicated for the kitchen.
- Place ribs in a large sealable plastic bag.
- For marinade, in a medium bowl combine 1 bottle of beer, olive oil, lemon juice, crumble bay leaf, kosher salt, garlic, cumin, onion powder and chili powder.
- Evenly coat the ribs, seal the bag and refrigerate overnight.
- Remove ribs from refrigerator 30 minutes prior to cooking.
- Drain ribs and discard the marinade. Sprinkle ribs with salt and pepper.
- Make 2 smoke pouches (see page 5).
- Prepare the barbecue for indirect smoking by adding the beer-filled drip pan to the unlit side, and oil the grill. Crank heat up on one side and place smoke pouch on the burner. Close the lid and wait for smoke.
- Once barbecue is smoking, place the ribs on the side of the barbecue without direct heat. Smoke the ribs over indirect heat for 2 1/2 hours, replacing the smoke pouch once and refilling the drip pan if necessary. If not, drink the remaining beer.
- Remove ribs from grill. Tent with foil and allow to rest for 15 minutes.

Serves 6–8

DRY JERK BABY BACK RIBS

Don't worry, "Jerk" does not refer to the person making the ribs. Jerk is a Jamaican spice rub that you can make on your own (way more fun than buying a bottle in the store). Adjust the flavors to suit your palate. Make a big batch and keep it in a dry place out of direct sunlight and it will last for a month at least without fading on you.

4 racks of pork baby back ribs

2 cups of dark rum (500ml)

1 cinnamon stick

Dry Jerk Rub

2 tbsp chili powder (30ml)

2 tbsp dried chives (30ml)

2 tbsp dried onion flakes (30ml)

2 tbsp coarse salt (30ml)

2 tsp ground coriander (10ml)

2 tsp ground ginger (10ml)

1 tsp freshly ground black pepper (5ml)

1 tsp ground allspice (5ml)

1/2 tsp ground cinnamon (2.5ml)

1/4 tsp ground cloves (1.25ml)

1/4 tsp ground nutmeg (1.25ml)

3 cups hickory flavored woodchips

Directions:

- Place the ribs, dark rum and cinnamon stick into large sealable plastic bags and let marinate for 3 hours in the refrigerator.

- Combine chili powder, chives, onion flakes, salt, coriander, ginger, black pepper, allspice, cinnamon, cloves and nutmeg and in a spice grinder (or mortar & pestle) and grind away until you have a fine powder.

- Drain ribs from marinade and pat dry with paper towel.

- Rub dry rub over ribs and place back into the fridge to finish marinating for at least 1 hour.

- Preheat the grill to high on one side. Leave the other burner off for indirect smoking with a drip pan underneath.

- Make 2 smoke pouches (see page 5).

- Place one of the pouches on the lit burner and close the lid. When you get smoke, reduce the heat to 220F/110C and place the ribs on the unlit side. Do this quickly so as not to loose any smoke.

- Close the lid and smoke for 2 hours (you'll need to change the smoke pouch after an hour or so) or until meat is very tender and has shrunk back from the ends of the bones.

Serves 4

JERK MANGO-GLAZED VEAL RIBS

Yes, that's right . . . veal ribs. Not quite as well known as pork or beef ribs, so your
dinner guests are going to sit up and take notice. Check out the marinade for this one.
There's about a thousand different flavors working together to make sure these are the
best ribs you've ever cooked.

2 4-lb racks of veal ribs (2 x 1.8 kg)

Marinade

8 whole green onions

2 tbsp fresh thyme leaves (30ml)

2 tsp ground allspice (10ml)

1 tsp salt (5ml)

2 tsp ground black pepper (10ml)

1 tsp nutmeg (5ml)

1 tsp cinnamon (5ml)

6 cloves garlic, finely minced

2 tbsp finely minced ginger (30ml)

*2 scotch bonnet peppers, seeds removed
    and finely minced*

1 cup mango puree (250ml)

4 tbsp mushroom flavored soy sauce (60ml)

2 tbsp cider vinegar (30ml)

1/2 cup vegetable oil (125ml)

1/2 cup dark rum (125ml)

Juice of 1 lime

Cherry wood chips for smoking

Directions:

- In a food processor combine all the marinade ingredients and blitz until a smooth paste is achieved.

- Set aside 1/2 cup (125ml) of the marinade for basting.

- Place the veal ribs on a large baking tray and pour marinade over the veal. Turn veal to make sure meat is entirely covered.

- Cover with plastic wrap and refrigerate overnight.

- Make 3 smoke pouches (see page 5).

- Prepare the barbecue for indirect grilling. Crank the heat on one side and place the first smoke pouch directly on the burner. Close the lid and wait for smoke. Once barbecue is smoking, reduce the heat to 220F/110C.

- Remove ribs from the marinade and pat dry 30 minutes before cooking.

- Place the ribs on cool side of barbecue opposite the smoke pouch.

- Close the lid, smoke for 3 hours. Change smoke pouch every hour or so.

- Baste with reserved marinade every 30 minutes.

- Place the ribs on a tray and tent loosely with foil and rest for 15 minutes before serving.

Serves 6

Lamb

Lamb & Fig Kabobs

Lamb Kabobs

Pumpkin Lamb Burgers with Tzatziki Topping

Asian Spiced Lamb Burgers with Plum Sauce

Blackberry Peppered Lamb Chops

Onion Water Lamb Chops

Smokin' Stuffed Leg of Lamb

Grilled Leg of Lamb

Port Marinated Racks of Lamb

Lamb Loin with Rosemary

Smoked Lamb Shanks with Hoisin Barbecue Sauce

Lamb Souvlaki

Grilled Lamb Ribs

LAMB & FIG KABOBS

Few things go as well together as port, figs and lamb. Please note you need fresh – not dried – figs. And don't cheap out on the red wine you use in the marinade. No, it doesn't have to be a $200 bottle of Chateau Smelly Socks but it should be something you'd like to drink. A good wine with this dish would be a nice zippy Zinfandel or a big Shiraz.

Cippolinis look like little onions but are actually bulbs from the grape hyacinth. Like you needed to know this. No cippolinis? Use shallots instead. Have your butcher debone the lamb leg for you.

2 1/4-lb boneless leg of lamb (1.2kg)

15 cippolini onions

10 black mission figs

1/2 cup port (125ml)

3 tbsp olive oil (45ml)

2 tsp cracked black pepper (10ml)

Directions:

- Place the leg of lamb on a cutting board and cut away the silver skin. Remove excess fat to avoid any nasty flare-ups.

- Cut the lamb into 1/2-inch cubes and place into a sealable plastic baggie.

Marinade

1 cup parsley, roughly chopped (250ml)

1 tbsp oregano, roughly chopped (15ml)

1 tbsp garlic, chopped fine (15ml)

1 shallot, minced fine

1/4 cup olive oil (60ml)

Juice of 1 lemon

Zest of 2 lemons, chopped fine

2 tsp pepper (10ml)

1/2 cup red wine (125ml)

Kosher salt to taste

Cracked pepper to taste

Olive oil for drizzling

14 wooden skewers soaked in water for
   at least an hour

- Toss the parsley, oregano, garlic and shallot in with the lamb. Pour in the olive oil, squeeze in some lemon juice, lemon zest and add the pepper and the red wine. Coat evenly and refrigerate overnight.

- Remove lamb from the refrigerator about 30 minutes before cooking.

- Remove lamb from baggie and discard marinade.

- Bring a large pot of water to a boil and add cippolinis. Cook for approximately 2 minutes. Remove and place in an ice bath to cool. Peel the skins off.

- Skewer the lamb cubes alternating with cippolini. Finish with a lamb cube. You should have 3 pieces of lamb and 2 cippolini per skewer. Repeat.

- Place on tray, drizzle with olive oil and season with salt and pepper.

- Slice figs in half and cover with port. Sprinkle with pepper and let stand for 15 minutes. Fit figs securely on to their own bamboo skewers. Drizzle with oil.

- Prepare barbecue for direct grilling. Preheat to medium-high heat. Oil the grill.

- Place the lamb skewers on the grill.

- Place a sheet of aluminum foil under the skewer ends that are exposed.

- Grill for 3 minutes per side for medium-rare or until desired doneness.

- Place the figs on grill for 2 minutes or until lightly charred. Note the high sugar content in the figs can burn easily so watch carefully.

Serves 6

LAMB KABOBS

Sweet molasses and tangy Dijon combined with rosemary (a classic lamb flavor boost) make for a very interesting kabob. This goes great with a pasta salad or grilled spuds.

3-lb leg of lamb, cubed (1.4Kg)

Marinade

2 tbsp Dijon (30ml)

1 tbsp molasses (15ml)

1 tbsp rosemary (15ml)

1 tsp dill (5ml)

1/4 cup olive oil (50ml)

1 tsp pepper (5ml)

1 onion, chopped

Bamboo skewers soaked in water for 1 hour

Directions:

- Place the marinade ingredients into a medium sized bowl and mix together.

- Place the lamb and marinade in a plastic bag and refrigerate for 2 hours. Remove from the fridge 30 minutes before cooking.

- Remove the lamb from the marinade. Skewer 4–5 lamb cubes per skewer.

- Preheat barbeque to medium-high heat.

- Oil grill and season lamb with salt and pepper.

- Place lamb skewers on grill for 6 minutes per side.

- Tent with tin foil for 10 minutes before serving.

Yield: 4–5 Skewers

PUMPKIN LAMB BURGERS WITH TZATZIKI TOPPING

Check this one out. Pumpkin pie spice mix generally consists of allspice, nutmeg, cinnamon and ginger – a combination that works really well with the ground lamb. Don't tell anyone and watch the love when they take the first bite. Tzatziki is the main ingredient in the topping and can be store bought. It's made of yogurt, cucumber, mint and garlic and is perfect on top of this burger. Make an extra big batch as it will keep in the fridge for a week and the flavors get better the longer it mellows.

Patties

1 1/2 lbs ground lamb sausage, squeezed
    from casings
1 cup chopped onions (250ml)
1 1/2 tsp salt (7ml)
1 1/2 tsp pumpkin pie spice (7ml)
1 tsp cayenne (5ml)

Tzatziki Topping

1 cup of diced plum tomatoes (250ml)
1/2 cup chives
1 tbsp balsamic vinegar
1 cup tzatziki

4 6-inch pita breads

Directions:

- Combine patty ingredients, and mix well.

- Using moistened hands, form 4 burgers

- Cover with plastic wrap and let marinate overnight.

- Preheat grill to medium high. Oil the grill

- Grill the burgers for about 7 minutes per side

- Mix the tomatoes with chopped chives and balsamic vinegar, then add to the tzatziki

- Cut 1/4-inch off of each pita. Serve lamb burgers in pita with a dollop of tzatziki topping.

Serves 4

ASIAN SPICED LAMB BURGERS WITH PLUM SAUCE

There are a few great store-bought plum sauces out there but most of them suck. Make your own. It's easy and you can play with the recipe until you get the flavor profile you like the best. Then bottle it, sell it, make a bazillion dollars, retire to your own island off the coast of Greece or something and invite me for dinner.

Patties

2 lbs ground lamb (1 kg)

4 tsp fish sauce (20ml)

1 tbsp fresh minced garlic (15ml)

1 tbsp lime zest (15ml)

2 tbsp cilantro (30ml)

2 tbsp chopped fresh basil (30ml)

Salt and pepper to taste

Plum sauce

5 fresh plums, sliced in wedges for
  approximately 2 cups

1 tbsp ginger chopped fine (15ml)

Juice of 1 orange

2 tbsp sugar (30ml)

1/2 red onion, chopped fine

1 tbsp rice wine vinegar (15ml)

Directions:

- Combine patty ingredients in a bowl and mix well. Refrigerate for at least 3 hours to set up.

- Remove from the refrigerator and make small lamb patties approximately 2-inches across. Place on a baking sheet.

- Combine all plum sauce ingredients in a saucepan.

- Set pot over medium heat and cook for 8 minutes.

- Remove from heat and cool to room temperature

- Prepare barbecue for direct grilling. Preheat the barbecue to medium-high heat. Oil the grill and place the burgers on the grill for approximately 5 minutes per side.

- Remove from grill and tent for 5 minutes with foil.

- Serve with plum sauce.

Serves 6–8

BLACKBERRY PEPPERED LAMB CHOPS

A "double cut" just means you cut the rack every second rib for a thicker chop. You can ask your butcher to do this for you if you'd like. This is one of the most interesting marinades we've ever come up with and believe me, in 104 episodes of *Licence To Grill* we've come up with lots. The combination of berries, port and mint work well with the slightly gamey flavor of the lamb. Please, do not overcook.

10 lamb rack chops, double cut
  (ask your butcher)
2 tbsp olive oil (30ml)
Salt and pepper to taste

Directions:

- In a bowl mash the blackberries with the tines of a fork.

- Add the chopped mint, cracked pink and black peppercorns, port and black pepper.

- Place lamb chops in a sealable plastic bag and cover with the marinade.

Blackberry Pink Peppercorn Marinade

2 pints blackberries

1/4 cup chopped mint (60ml)

1 tbsp pink peppercorns cracked (15ml)

1 cup port (250ml)

2 tsp black peppercorns cracked (10ml)

- Put in the refrigerator to marinate for 3 hours. Remove from the fridge 30 minutes before grilling.

- Prepare the barbecue for direct grilling. Preheat the grill to medium heat. Oil grill.

- Remove lamb from baggie and discard excess marinade. Pat dry with paper towels. Season with salt and drizzle with oil.

- Wrap the exposed bones in foil. This will prevent them from burning, which gives the lamb a bitter flavor.

- Place seasoned lamb on the grill.

- Grill for 3 minutes per side or until nice char marks and deep caramelization is achieved. Watch closely to prevent burning.

- Remove from the grill and tent with tin foil for 10 minutes before serving.

Serves 5

ONION WATER LAMB CHOPS

This is possibly *the best* lamb chop recipe we've come up with. It is absolutely my favorite as I love the way the onion water infuses the lamb meat. Very yummy. Very easy.

8 loin lamb chops (each 4– 5 oz and
    1 1/2-inch thick)

1/3 tsp saffron threads (1.5ml)

1 tbsp hot water (15ml)

2 lbs onions, chopped

2 leeks, chopped, white part only

1 tsp ground turmeric (5ml)

2 tsp celery salt (10ml)

1 tbsp garlic salt (15ml)

1 jalapeno, chopped

Salt and pepper to taste

Directions:

- In a small bowl add the saffron and hot water, let sit for 2 1/2 minutes to steep.

- In a blender, mix half of the onions and half the leeks. Blitz.

- Once they have started to come together add remaining onions and leek and blend. Strain this mixture into a bowl.

- Strain the saffron into the bowl as well.

- Add turmeric, celery salt and garlic salt and stir it all together.

- Place the lamb chops into a sealable plastic bag. Pour marinade over the lamb. Add jalapeno pepper. Refrigerate for 2 1/2 hours. Remove from the fridge a good 30 minutes before grilling.

- Preheat the barbecue to high heat.

- Remove the lamb from marinade and place onto an oiled grill.

- Season the chops with salt and pepper and keep some water handy in case of flare ups on the grill. Barbecue the chops for approximately 3–5 minutes per side.

- Tent with tin foil for 5 minutes before serving.

Serves 4

SMOKIN' STUFFED LEG OF LAMB

I know, I know . . . I keep saying you gotta cook with the bone in whenever you can. But this time, you get to stuff the lamb and then smoke it 'til it's nice and tender and the cheese has melted inside with the pine nuts and spinach. And the aroma . . . oh, your gonna love the smells coming off that barbecue about an hour into the cooking. Get a big stick to beat everyone off as they try and see what's going on under the lid.

5 –5 1/2 lbs boned leg of lamb (2.5Kg)

1 clove garlic, sliced into 4 pieces

Salt and pepper

Marinade

10 garlic cloves

Juice and zest of one lemon

2 tbsp brown sugar (30ml)

1 1/2 tbsp olive oil (22ml)

Directions:

- To prepare the marinade, add first three ingredients to a mini food processor. Start the processor and gradually add oil to the mixture until thick and emulsified.

- Place the lamb in a large sealable bag and pour the marinade overtop. Shake bag so the meat is thoroughly coated. Place meat in the refrigerator and marinate overnight, up to 24 hours. Take the lamb out of the fridge an hour before smoking.

Stuffing

1 tbsp olive oil (15ml)

2 garlic cloves, sliced in half

1/2 medium onion, chopped

1/3 cup pine nuts (75ml)

1 1/2 lbs fresh spinach or packaged
   frozen spinach

1/3 cup chopped fresh parsley (75ml)

8 ounces mild goat cheese

1/4 cup dried cranberries (60ml)

1 tsp Worcestershire sauce (5ml)

Salt and pepper to taste

Drip pan

1 cup white wine (250ml)

3 sprigs rosemary

- To prepare the stuffing, heat oil in a skillet, add chopped garlic and onions and sauté for a few minutes until soft. Add pine nuts and stir. After a few more minutes, scrape the onions, garlic, and pine nuts mixture into a large bowl.

- Clean the spinach. Bring a large pot of salted water to a boil. Add spinach to the water for 30 seconds. Remove the spinach and run under cold water. Pat dry. Chop spinach and add to the pine nut mixture in the large bowl. If using pre-cooked frozen spinach, defrost and squeeze the excess moisture out before placing in the bowl. Add the parsley, goat cheese, dried cranberries, Worcestershire sauce, salt, pepper and mash together.

- Remove the leg of lamb from marinade and pat dry. Slice 4 slits through the leg and stuff one garlic slice into each. Season cavity with salt and pepper.

- Stuff the leg of lamb with the filling and close the meat around the filling. Secure the roast with butcher twine.

- To prepare lamb for grilling, place in a skillet with hot oil and sear meat 1-2 minutes on each side.

- Pour wine in drip pan and add rosemary.

- Remove the grill from one side of the barbeque and insert drip pan. Replace grill.

- Preheat the other side of the grill to 220C/104F.

- Place lamb on grill above the drip pan and cook for 30 minutes per pound.

- Replenish wine in drip pan as necessary.

- Remove lamb from grill, cover with foil and let rest for 20 minutes before serving.

Serves 6

GRILLED LEG OF LAMB

For some reason, I find white wine works better in a lamb marinade than red (although you'd drink red with the lamb – go figure). The recipe calls for 6 garlic cloves but go ahead and add a ton more if you'd like. Remember, barbecue is an art, not a science so messing with recipes is not only allowed, it's encouraged.

1 5-lb leg of lamb, bone-in (2.2kg)

1/3 cup olive oil (80ml)

2/3 cup white wine (150ml)

6 cloves garlic, finely chopped

2 tbsp chopped fresh oregano, plus sprigs
*   for garnish (45ml)*

1 tbsp chopped thyme (15ml)

Salt to taste

Freshly ground coarse pepper to taste

Juice of 2 lemons and the zest, chopped fine

Directions:

* Place the leg of lamb in a glass dish and drizzle with olive oil and wine, add garlic, oregano, thyme, salt and pepper lemon juice and lemon zest. Be sure to coat the lamb all over. Cover with plastic wrap or transfer to a large sealable plastic bag and refrigerate overnight.

* Remove from the refrigerator 1 hour before grilling.

* Prepare grill for direct grilling over medium heat.

* Remove the lamb from the marinade and pat dry with paper towel.

* Grill the meat directly over the heat elements for 1 1/2 hours or until desired doneness, turning halfway through.

* Check for doneness with an instant-read thermometer; it should register 130F /54C while resting. Tent the lamb with aluminum foil and let it rest for 20 minutes.

* Thinly slice, and serve immediately.

Serves 8

PORT MARINATED RACKS OF LAMB

The rack is probably the easiest and fastest cut of lamb to prepare on the barbecue. It has flavor from the bone, nice fat marbling and a pronounced lamb taste. Delicious. Less than 15 minutes on the grill and you're done which is just enough time to whip up a salad and some cocktails before your guests arrive. Perfect chichi weeknight dinner. Three racks easily serve 6 people. This marinade calls for a big boozy port to bump up the flavor even more. Get your butcher to remove the chine bone and French the rack for you.

3 racks of lamb, chine bones removed,

    racks Frenched

Marinade

1/4 cup plus 1 tbsp olive oil (60ml plus 15ml)

1/2 cup ruby port (125ml)

1/4 cup red wine vinegar (60ml)

1/4 cup fresh lemon juice (60ml)

1/4 cup whole grain Dijon mustard (60ml)

3 tbsp rosemary, finely chopped (45ml)

1 tbsp coarsely cracked black pepper (15ml)

1 tbsp fresh garlic (15ml)

2 tbsp shallots, minced (30ml)

1 tbsp of brown sugar (15ml)

Salt and pepper to taste

Directions:

- Place the racks of lamb into a sealable plastic bag.

- In a large glass or ceramic (non-reactive) bowl, combine 1/4 cup olive oil with rest of the marinade ingredients. Mix together and pour into the bag over the lamb.

- Seal the bag and place it in the fridge to marinate for 2 hours. Take the racks out of the fridge 30 minutes before grilling.

- Preheat the grill to 375F/187C.

- Remove the lamb from the marinade and scrape off as much of the liquid as possible, then pat dry with paper towel.

- Rub the lamb with the remaining 1 tbsp of olive oil and season with salt and pepper.

- Wrap the Frenched bones of the lamb in tin foil.

- Oil the grill and place the lamb meat-side down for 6 minutes with the lid up. Move meat away from any flare ups that may occur.

- Flip and continue to grill for another 6 minutes or until internal temperature reaches 130F/65C (medium rare).

- Let the lamb rest for 5 minutes under a foil tent and remove the foil from the bones before serving.

Serves 6

LAMB LOIN WITH ROSEMARY

A lamb loin is the same cut as a rack but without the bones. It's juicy and easy to prepare. Absolutely positively tent with foil for at least 5 minutes before serving and slice into medallions.

5 tbsp extra-virgin olive oil (75ml)

1/4 cup dry red wine (60ml)

1 1/2 tbsp chopped fresh rosemary (22.5ml)
  or 2 tsp dried (10ml)

2 large garlic cloves, pressed

2 small shallots, diced

1/2 tsp salt (2.5ml)

1/2 tsp ground black pepper (2.5ml)

2 lamb loins

Fresh rosemary sprigs

Directions:

- Whisk oil, wine, diced shallots, rosemary, garlic, salt and pepper in a bowl.

- Place the lamb loins in a large plastic sealable bag, pour marinade over the meat and coat.

- Let stand at room temperature for 1 hour or refrigerate for 4-6 hours. Remove from the fridge at least 30 minutes before grilling.

- Preheat grill to medium-high heat. Don't forget to oil the grill.

- Remove the lamb from marinade, shaking off excess and pat dry with paper towel.

- Season the lamb with salt and pepper. Grill lamb to desired doneness, about 4 minutes per side (depending on thickness) for medium-rare.

- Transfer to a platter and tent with tin foil for 5 minutes.

- Slice into medallions, garnish with rosemary springs and serve.

Serves 4

SMOKED LAMB SHANKS WITH HOISIN BARBECUE SAUCE

The superb lamb shank is a tougher cut of meat that requires long slow cooking with lots of liquid until it's practically falling off the bone and every mouthful is a sublime taste experience that makes the eyes roll back in your head and you go, "Oh man, gimme more of that!" Chinese five-spice is a combination of cinnamon, cloves, fennel, star anise and peppercorns. You can find it in any good grocery store or make your own.

Hoisin is a sweet and spicy Chinese condiment made from soybeans, garlic, chili peppers and a bunch of spices. It's also called "Peking" sauce in some places and is a killer accompaniment to the lamb when combined with barbecue sauce (your own concoction or store bought if you'd like) and applesauce. Enjoy.

6 lamb shanks

1/4 cup sesame oil (60ml)

Rub

1 tbsp salt (15ml)

1 tbsp sugar (15ml)

1 tsp black pepper (5ml)

1 tsp Chinese five-spice (5ml)

Hoisin Barbecue Sauce

1/2 cup barbeque sauce (125ml)

1/2 cup Hoisin sauce (125ml)

2 tbsp rice wine vinegar (30ml)

1 tbsp hot sauce (15ml)

2 tbsp of applesauce (30ml)

Hickory wood chips for smoking

Directions:

- Rub the shanks with the sesame oil.

- In a small bowl, mix together salt, sugar, pepper and Chinese five-spice.

- Rub mixture over lamb shanks evenly. Let sit at room temperature under plastic wrap for 1 hour or in the fridge for 4 hours. Remove from the fridge at least 30 minutes before cooking.

- Make a smoke pouch (see page 5).

- Prepare barbecue for indirect grilling. Crank heat on one side and place the smoke pouch directly on burner. Close lid and wait for smoke, then reduce the heat to 220F/110C

- Once temperature is reached, place lamb shanks over the unlit side of grill. Close lid of barbeque.

- Smoke the lamb for one hour.

- Meanwhile, mix together the Hoisin Barbecue Sauce ingredients in a medium size bowl.

- After 1 hour remove the lamb, and place on a baking tray with high sides.

- Brush each lamb shank with the Hoisin Barbecue Sauce.

- Cover the shanks loosely in tin foil. Seal package well and return to the unlit side of the barbecue

- Close the lid and cook for 1 hour.

- Remove the lamb from grill. Let it cool slightly and remove foil. The lamb should almost fall off the bone. Transfer the lamb (carefully – use tongs and a spatula) to a platter and tent with foil for 10 minutes

- Serve with additional Hoisin Barbecue Sauce.

Serves 6

LAMB SOUVLAKI

"Souvlaki" is the name of an ancient Greek general who convinced the invading hordes to lay down their arms in return for lamb barbecued on the end of their spears. Kidding. Actually, the word originally meant the skewer and not that which is skewered there upon. It is a classic Greek dish (See? I told you *everyone* barbecues!) with a simple marinade that features yogurt, mint, garlic, lemon and lime (optional) juice. Note the recipe calls for the lean lamb loin so cooking time is short.

2 lbs trimmed lamb loin, cut into
   1-inch cubes (0.9Kg)
1 tbsp olive oil for brushing
Salt and pepper to taste

Marinade
1 cup yogurt (250ml)
4 tbsp chopped mint (60ml)
2 tbsp garlic, minced (30ml)
Zest of 1 lemon
Juice of 1 lime
3 tbsp olive oil (45ml)
1 tsp cracked pepper (5ml)

6 wooden skewers soaked in cool water
   1 hour prior to grilling

Directions:

- Combine marinade ingredients in a bowl and mix well.

- Place cubed lamb in a sealable plastic bag. Pour marinade over lamb.

- Seal the bag and refrigerate for at least 6 hours and overnight is even better.

- Remove the lamb from the fridge a good 30 minutes before cooking.

- Wipe off the marinade and pat the lamb dry with paper towel.

- Thread the lamb cubes evenly onto 6 soaked bamboo skewers. Season lamb with salt and pepper and brush with olive oil. Wrap foil around the bit of the skewer that remains uncovered.

- Preheat barbeque to medium high and oil the grill

- For medium-rare lamb grill for 3 minutes per side for a total of 6 minutes cooking time, or until desired doneness.

- Remove lamb from the grill and loosely cover with foil. Let meat rest for 10 minutes before serving.

Yield: 6 skewers

GRILLED LAMB RIBS

No one ever thinks of lamb ribs. They're small and have a decent amount of fat
(which is a good thing). There's not a lot of meat but what's there is perfect for the
barbecue. Plus, think of the look on your guests' faces when you tell them what
they're hoovering back.

3 1/2 lbs lamb ribs (1.59kg) with lots
   of fat (ask your butcher)

2 onions, chopped fine

2 tsp minced garlic (10ml)

1 tbsp chopped fresh oregano (15ml)

2 tsp chopped thyme (10ml)

1 tbsp liquid honey (15ml)

1/4 cup olive oil (60ml)

1 cup dry white wine (250ml)

1 tsp ground black pepper (5ml)

1 tsp ground cinnamon (5ml)

1 tbsp finely chopped lemon zest (15ml)

1/4 cup fresh lemon juice (60ml)

Cracked pepper and kosher salt to taste

Directions:

- To make the marinade mix in a small bowl the onion, garlic, oregano, thyme, honey, olive oil, white wine, pepper, cinnamon, lemon zest and lemon juice.

- Pour into baggie with ribs, reserving 1/3 cup (80ml) for basting later.

- Refrigerate overnight. Remove from the fridge at least 30 minutes before cooking. Discard excess marinade and season liberally with salt and pepper.

- Preheat the barbecue to 220F/110C with one side turned off for indirect cooking.

- Place the ribs on the side of the barbecue without direct heat.

- Cook with the barbecue lid closed for 1 1/2–2 hours or until tender.

- With 15 minutes of cooking time remaining, lift barbecue lid and drizzle ribs with reserved marinade.

- Tent the ribs with tin foil for 10 minutes before serving.

Serves 6

Vegetables & Fruit

Stuffed Grilled Zucchini

Twice-Grilled Potatoes

Spicy Grilled Potato Skins

Curried Roast Potatoes

Grilled Potatoes with Herbs

Rosemary Smoked Potatoes

Balsamic Grilled Mushrooms

Mushroom Kabobs

Portobello Cheeseburgers

Stuffed Smoked Onions

Grilled Bacon Onion Wedges

Grilled Onions with Spiced Summer Apricot Mustard Glaze

Cauliflower Kabobs

Charred Stuffed Jalapeno

Grilled Rice Cakes

Grilled Veggie Cornboats

Grilled Vegetables with Garlic Anchovy Dip

Marinated Carrots, Pearl Onions & Radishes

Smoked Corn on the Cob

Grilled Corn with Chipotle-Maple Glaze

Roasted Stuffed Pears

Smoked Acorn Squash with Maple Spiced Butter

Grilled Fennel with Garlic Anchovy Butter

Grilled Antipasto

Grilled Asparagus & Beets

Grilled Honey-Tarragon Carrots

STUFFED GRILLED ZUCCHINI

There are all sorts of "zukes" out there. For this recipe go for the ones that are about 6 inches long. Check the outer skin and make sure it's free of nicks and blemishes. Zucchini holds up nicely on the grill. No, you can't use dried herbs instead of fresh for this one . . .

1 tbsp extra-virgin olive oil (15ml)

1 cup finely chopped red onion (250ml)

1 tsp minced garlic (5ml)

1/2 cup dried bread crumbs (125ml)

1 tbsp finely chopped fresh oregano (15ml)

1 tbsp finely chopped chives (15ml)

1/2 tsp kosher salt (2.5 ml)

1/2 tsp fresh cracked pepper (2.5 ml)

3 medium zucchinis, trimmed and cut
    in half lengthwise

2 tbsp olive oil (30ml)

1 tbsp lemon zest (15ml)

1 cup grated mozzarella cheese (250ml)

1/4 cup freshly grated Parmigiano
    Reggiano cheese (125ml)

1/2 cup chopped red pepper (125ml)

Salt and pepper to taste

Directions:

- In a sauté pan set over medium heat, heat the oil.

- Add the onion and garlic. Sauté until translucent but not browned, about 3 to 4 minutes. Remove from heat and add bread crumbs, herbs, salt and pepper. Mix until combined. Place in a bowl to cool.

- Season zucchinis with salt and pepper and drizzle with oil.

- Prepare barbecue for direct grilling at a medium-high heat.

- Oil grill and place the zucchinis flesh-side down on grill for 3 minutes or until nicely charred. Remove.

- Allow zucchinis to cool slightly.

- Use a melon baller to scoop out centers, leaving a 1/2-inch border.

- Chop the zucchini flesh and add it to the bowl of onions and breadcrumbs. Mix well. Add cheese and diced red pepper to mixture.

- Add the filling back into the zucchini shells.

- Oil the grill and place zucchinis stuffing-side up on grill to cook for 8 minutes with the lid down or until filling is warm and cheese has turned golden brown.

Serves 6

TWICE-GRILLED POTATOES

We love grilling potatoes so much, we do it *twice* in the same recipe. Har har.
Actually the reason for the double grilling is to soften up the spud enough to scoop
the flesh out, then mix with all the great stuff below and then return to the barbecue
to warm through. This is a killer side with steak or chicken.

4 russet potatoes, cleaned

2 tbsp vegetable oil (30ml)

Salt and pepper

Directions:

- Wash the potatoes, pat dry with paper towel and cut in half lengthwise.

- Rub with oil and season with salt and pepper.

Stuffing

1/2 cup whipped cream (125ml)

1/2 cup grated provolone cheese (125ml)

1/2 cup grated Parmesan cheese (125ml)

3 tbsp chopped chives in 1" pieces (45ml)

1/2 cup cooked bacon (125ml)

2 tbsp Dijon mustard (30ml)

Salt and pepper to taste

1/2 cup sour cream to garnish (125ml)

- Prepare barbecue for direct grilling at low heat. Oil the grill well and place the potatoes flesh-side down. Close the barbecue lid and cook for 30 minutes, turning once until soft and flesh side is caramelized. Remove from grill and cool slightly.

- Scoop out the insides leaving a 1/2-inch (1.75 cm) border all around the potato so that it won't fall apart on the grill.

- Place the scooped potato in a bowl and add whip cream and half of the cheese.

- Add the chives, bacon, Dijon, salt and pepper. Mix the stuffing until well combined, but still chunky.

- Fill the potatoes with stuffing and top with the remaining cheese.

- Place back on grill at medium low heat.

- Cook until warmed through and cheese has caramelized. Approximately 7 – 10 minutes. Remove and top with sour cream. Enjoy!

Yield: 8 halves

SPICY GRILLED POTATO SKINS

I've got to be honest with you, I'm not a big fan of potato skins but everyone else seems to love them and all the flavor *is* in the skin after all and not so much the flesh. Here's our take on the roadhouse standby. Enjoy.

6 baking potatoes (4–6 oz each /113g –170g)

1 tbsp vegetable oil (15ml)

3/4 cup bottled salsa (180ml)

1 cup sour cream (250ml)

1 tbsp finely chopped jalapeno (15ml)

1 tbsp roasted garlic (15ml)

1 cup grated cheddar (250ml)

1/4 cup chives cut into 1 inch (16cm)
pieces to garnish (60ml)

Directions:

- Wash potatoes well and pat dry with paper towel.

- Using the tines of a fork, prick potatoes all over. Wrap potatoes in aluminum foil.

- Preheat barbecue to 300F/150C and cook potatoes with the lid down for 40 minutes or until tender.

- Remove the spuds from the grill. Unwrap the foil and slice them in half.

- Scoop the flesh out of the potatoes leaving approximately 1/2 an inch (1.27cm) of the flesh around the sides. Allow to cool. Brush the skins with oil and season with salt and pepper.

- Place the skins on well oiled preheated medium-high grill for 8 minutes flesh-side down or until golden and crispy. Remove.

- Lay the potato skins out in a row and drop a dollop of bottled salsa in each, followed by sour cream and then chopped jalapeno and roasted garlic.

- Add grated cheddar and top with chopped chives.

- Serve right away

Serves 6

CURRIED ROAST POTATOES

I do love potatoes on the barbecue. Technically you could do these on the stove but hey, it's too hot in the summer, so get outside and fire up the grill.

1 large vidalia onion cut into large wedges

2 tsp ground coriander (10ml)

2 tsp ground cumin (10ml)

1/2 tsp cayenne pepper (2ml)

3 tsp curry powder (15ml)

1 tsp turmeric (5ml)

3 tsp freshly grated ginger (15ml)

1 1/2 tsp crushed garlic (7ml)

Salt and pepper to taste

3 cups chicken broth (750ml)

6 potatoes unpeeled, washed and quartered

2 limes quartered

1 tbsp vegetable oil (30ml)

Directions:

- Preheat the grill to medium high.

- Place a large cast iron skillet on the grill to heat up for 3 or 4 minutes.

- Add the onions and cook without oil and without stirring for 8 minutes or until the onions begin to brown.

- Add spices, ginger, garlic, salt and pepper and cook until fragrant, maybe 2 or 3 minutes longer.

- Add 1 1/2 cups (450ml) of chicken stock and stir, picking up the onion bits from the bottom of the pan. Simmer over low heat for approximately 10–15 minutes until the mixture gets thick and the stock reduces.

- Add the potatoes to the mixture and toss to coat.

- Add the remaining stock.

- Place the skillet uncovered on the grill and close the lid.

- Cook for 30 minutes adding water/stock as necessary or until potatoes are tender.

Serves 6

GRILLED POTATOES WITH HERBS

Obviously you can play with the type of herbs you want to use in this recipe. The trick is not to cut the spuds too thick or they will burn on the grill before cooking all the way through.

3 Yukon Gold potatoes

3 tbsp olive oil (45ml)

1 tsp dried thyme (5ml)

2 tsp dried oregano (10ml)

Salt and pepper to taste

Directions:

- Slice potatoes 1/2-inch thick and place into a sealable plastic bag. Add oil, dried thyme, oregano, salt and pepper. Seal the bag and toss the potatoes to ensure they are well coated. Set aside.

- Preheat barbecue to medium-low heat.

- Oil the grill liberally. Remove the potatoes from the bag and place them directly over the heat. Cook for approximately 8 minutes per side or until golden brown, crispy and cooked through.

Serves 4

ROSEMARY SMOKED POTATOES

If you want even more flavor, parboil the spuds in chicken stock instead of water. Parboil just means boiling them 'til they soften up a bit as opposed to all the way through (otherwise they might fall apart on the grill).

15 small red skinned baby potatoes

8 rosemary stalks, soaked in water for
    30 minutes

2 tbsp garlic, chopped (30ml)

1/4 cup oil (60ml)

Salt and pepper to taste

Directions:

- Parboil the potatoes whole in salted water for 10 minutes. Allow to cool and drain.

- Halve the potatoes and place in a plastic bag. Drizzle with oil and chopped garlic. Seal bag and let marinate at room temperature for 20 minutes.

- Soak the rosemary sprigs in water.

- Preheat barbecue to 325F/162C

- Remove the potatoes from marinade; discard any excess marinade.

- Season the potatoes with salt and pepper.

- Place the soaked rosemary on the grate. Place the potatoes on top of the rosemary. Close the lid and leave to smoke for 15 minutes.

- Remove the potatoes and discard the charred rosemary.

Serves 6

BALSAMIC GRILLED MUSHROOMS

'Shrooms and balsamic are a classic combo. This side works well with chicken or steak. Bit too much for fish though.

2 lbs button mushrooms, cleaned

3 tbsp balsamic vinegar

1/4 cup olive oil

Salt and pepper to taste

Directions:

- Place a grill basket on the barbecue and heat on high for 15 minutes with the lid closed.

- Toss all of the ingredients into a large bowl to coat.

- Place the mushrooms directly into the hot grill basket.

- Toss and turn the mushrooms every 2 minutes until they are golden brown and evenly cooked.

Serves 6

MUSHROOM KABOBS

Don't marinate for more than 20 minutes or the 'shrooms will go moosh. Make sure the mushrooms are all about the same size to ensure even cooking time.

1 lb of whole button mushrooms, cleaned
    and stems trimmed (450g)

12 bamboo skewers, soaked in water for a
    minimum of 30 minutes

Marinade

1/2 cup dry red wine (125ml)

1/4 cup olive oil (62ml)

1 tbsp lemon juice (15ml)

2 large cloves garlic, minced

3 tsp dried thyme

1 tsp sea or kosher salt (5ml)

1 tsp freshly cracked black pepper (5ml)

Directions:

- Place the mushrooms in a large plastic bag.

- Combine all of the marinade ingredients and pour over the mushrooms. Seal the bag and marinate for 20 minutes at room temperature.

- Preheat the grill to high heat.

- Remove the mushrooms from the bag and discard the marinade.

- Skewer the mushrooms and place them onto the grill.

- Grill for approximately 7–10 minutes with the lid up and turning on a regular basis to ensure even cooking.

Serves 6

PORTOBELLO CHEESEBURGERS

"Portobello" seems to be Italian for "really nice door you have there." Apparently some marketing whiz came up with the name in the 1980s to help sell these big mother 'shrooms. Looks like it worked. Portobellos hold up really well on the grill because of their size and density. Enjoy.

4 large portobello mushroom caps, cleaned

1/4 cup balsamic vinegar (62ml)

2 tbsp olive oil (30ml)

1 tsp dried basil (5ml)

1 tsp dried oregano (5ml)

1 tbsp minced garlic (15ml)

Salt and pepper to taste

4 slices mozzarella cheese

Directions:

- Place the mushrooms in a large plastic bag.

- Add the balsamic vinegar, olive oil, basil, oregano, garlic and salt and pepper.

- Marinate at room temperature for 15 minutes

- Preheat the grill to high heat.

- Oil the grill and place the mushrooms top-side down on the grill and cook for 2 minutes. Flip and cook for another 2 minutes.

- Flip again and add a slice of cheese to each mushroom.

- Continue to cook for another 2–3 minutes until the cheese is melted and the mushrooms are tender and cooked through.

Serves 4

STUFFED SMOKED ONIONS

Get vidalia onions if they're in season. They are sweeter and milder but a good Spanish onion will do just as well.

6 large Spanish or vidalia onions (8oz ea)

1 cup bread crumbs (250ml)

2/3 cup chicken broth (175 ml)

1 lb fresh veal sausage

1 tsp dried oregano (5ml)

1 tsp dried sage (5ml)

1/2 tsp dried cumin (2ml)

3 tbsp pine nuts (45ml)

Make a smoke pouch (see page 5)

3 cups apple wood chips

3 sprigs fresh thyme

Directions:

- Leave the outer papery skin on the onions, wash and rinse.

- Trim the root end off onion to make a flat bottom. Cut tops off and reserve.

- Hollow out the centers leaving two or three outer layers in tact. Reserve center for other use.

- In a bowl, mix remaining ingredients. Toss gently to combine. Fill onions with equal amounts of sausage mix. Place tops on onions.

- Place each onion upright in center of a piece of heavy-duty aluminum foil and bring edges up to seal. Seal loosely to allow steam to escape.

- Prepare the barbecue for indirect grilling. Crank the heat on one side and place the smoke pouch directly on the burner. Close the lid and wait for smoke. Once barbecue is smoking, reduce the heat to 220F/110C

- Place the onion parcels upright on the unlit side, close the lid and cook for an hour or until very tender.

- Remove the onions from foil and carefully remove the outermost skin. Whoa baby, that's hot! Watch your fingers.

- Reserve cooking juices and drizzle over the onions.

Serves 6

GRILLED BACON ONION WEDGES

Another cool variation on this recipe is to wrap the onion wedges in prosciutto instead of regular bacon.

2 large sweet onions, cut into wedges

8 thick slices bacon

2 tbsp balsamic vinegar (30ml)

2 tbsp brown sugar (30ml)

1 tbsp molasses (15ml)

Bamboo skewers soaked in water

Directions:

- Wrap the onion wedges in bacon and fasten them on with soaked bamboo skewers. Place them into a large sealable plastic bag. Add balsamic, sugar and molasses and toss gently to coat.

- Marinate for 30 minutes or so at room temperature.

- Preheat barbecue to medium-high heat and oil grill

- Remove the onions from the marinade. Pat dry with paper towels.

- Place them on the grill to barbecue for approximately 8–10 minutes per side. Keep an eye on them as you'll probably get flare ups as the bacon begins to cook and the fat drips so you'll have to move them around. No problem here as you're not going for nice char marks.

Serves 6

GRILLED ONIONS WITH SPICED SUMMER APRICOT MUSTARD GLAZE

A nice Spanish onion will do in a pinch if vidalia onions are out of season. The Dijon, lemon juice and vinegar add tartness to the sweet apricot jelly.

3 medium sweet vidalia onions

1 tbsp olive oil (15ml)

Apricot Mustard Glaze

2 cups apricot jelly (500ml)

2 tbsp Dijon mustard (30ml)

Juice of 3 lemons

1 tbsp rice wine vinegar (15ml)

1 shallot, chopped fine

Directions:

- Peel and slice the onion into approximately 1/4-inch-thick slices, brush both sides with olive oil. Place them on a baking sheet, ready for grill.

- Prepare barbecue for direct grilling. Preheat grill to medium heat.

- Oil grill and place onions on to cook for 3 minutes.

- Flip the onions over and baste with the apricot glaze and continue to cook a further 2–3 minutes.

Apricot Mustard Glaze Directions:

- Combine ingredients in a saucepan set over low heat.

- Simmer on low heat for 5 minutes and remove.

- Reserve half for a dipping sauce.

Serves 6–8

CAULIFLOWER KABOBS

Red curry paste has an amazingly deep and complex taste along with some great heat. Once you've tried this recipe you'll never think of cauliflower the same way again. Perfect as a side to a nicely grilled bit of salmon or tuna.

A head of cauliflower

2 tsp salt (5ml)

2 tsp red curry paste (10ml)

1 tsp sugar (5ml)

1/2 cup coconut milk (125ml)

Juice of 1 lime

6 10-inch (25cm) wooden bamboo skewers
   soaked in cool water 1 hour prior to grilling

Aluminum foil

Directions:

- Using a small pairing knife, cut the cauliflower from its core into 2-inch (5cm) florets.

- In a large pot set over high heat, boil 10 cups (2.5L) of salted water.

- Add the cauliflower to boiling water and cook for 3 minutes.

- Strain cauliflower in a colander and immediately plunge into an ice bath. This is done to prevent further cooking and to keep the cauliflower crisp. Once cool, strain from ice water bath and pat dry.

- In a small bowl mix red curry paste, sugar, coconut milk and the lime juice.

- Skewer the cauliflower florets on wooden skewers. Brush with the sauce.

- Preheat grill to medium high.

- Oil the grill and place a 4-inch (10cm) by 10-inch (25cm) piece of aluminum foil in the center of barbecue.

- Place the cauliflower directly on the grill with the ends of the skewers directly over foil. (This is to prevent burning of skewers.)

- Cook the florets while basting with sauce for 5 minutes or until golden brown char marks are achieved.

Yield: 6 kabobs

CHARRED STUFFED JALEPENO

Look for jalapenos clear of nicks and blemishes. This recipe requires you to "pipe" the stuffing into the charred pepper. If you don't have a piping bag, then put the cream cheese stuffing into a sturdy plastic bag and cut off one of the corners. Voila. Instant piping bag.

14 large jalapenos

1 tbsp olive oil (15ml)

1 package cream cheese (250g),
    room temperature

4 slices of bacon, fried crisp and crumbled

1 tbsp fresh oregano (15ml)

1/2 cup fresh chives, minced fine (125ml)

2 green onion, minced fine

Zest of 1 lemon

Salt and pepper to taste

Directions:

- Using a sharp knife, cut along the length of the jalapeno (being careful not to cut through to the other side) to create a pocket. Leave tops intact.

- Using the knife carefully devein and remove seeds from the chilies.

- Toss the jalapenos with olive oil.

- Preheat barbecue to medium-high heat.

- Place the chilies on grill and char on the outside for about 3 minutes turning constantly with tongs. Remove from grill and cool.

- When peppers are cool remove the charred skins and discard. You might want to wear rubber gloves for this part or at least remember: *do not* rub your eyes.

- In a medium bowl combine the cream cheese with the remaining ingredients and mix well. Place the mixture in a piping bag. Pipe the mixture into the peeled peppers.

- Preheat barbecue to 400F/204C or high heat. Place peppers on warming rack and allow the filling in peppers to get warm and gooey.

- Remove and let cool slightly before serving.

Yield: 14 peppers

GRILLED RICE CAKES

Tired of potatoes as a side dish? Check this one out. Grilled rice cakes go really well with fish or a nicely grilled pork tenderloin. No ring molds? Go to your local hardware store and get the guy to cut you some different widths of PVC pipe. Instant ring molds.

3 cups sushi rice, cooked following
  package instructions
1/4 cup rice wine vinegar (60ml)
1 tbsp sugar (15ml)
1 tsp salt (5ml)
1/4 cup chopped fresh basil (60ml)
3 tbsp lightly toasted pine nuts (45ml)
2 tbsp peanut oil for brushing (30ml)

Directions:

- Placed cooked warm rice in a bowl.

- In another bowl, mix together the rice wine vinegar, sugar and salt. Stir to dissolve.

- Pour the mixture over the rice and gently toss.

- Add the basil and pine nuts and mix until evenly distributed.

- Mold the rice into a 3-inch ring mold until it is about 3/4 inch in height. Gently pack in until a nice firm disk is achieved.

- *Tip: To stop rice from sticking to your hands, dip your hands in cold water before handling the rice.*

- Remove from the ring and place on a well-oiled baking sheet. Repeat and brush the cakes with the peanut oil.

- Preheat the barbecue to medium heat.

- Oil the grill and place the rice cakes on direct heat.

- Grill for approximately 3 minutes per side or until nice golden crispy char marks are achieved.

- Remove from heat. Plate and serve.

Makes 8 cakes

GRILLED VEGGIE CORNBOATS

This looks way more complicated than it really is. I promise that once you've tried it, this will become a favorite side. Try adding different veggies depending on your personal tastes. Smoked gouda is a great cheese that doesn't get as big a workout as some of the more popular types.

6 cobs of corn

2 red peppers

2 yellow peppers

20 asparagus stems, woody part
   of stem removed

Directions:

- Preheat the grill to high.

- Pull the husks back from the cob without tearing them off. Remove the silk from the corn.

- Using a paring knife, carefully remove the cob of corn from the husks which should remain intact and attached by the end of the cob. Place the husks into a pot of water to soak.

10 cloves garlic with the skin on

2 red onions, cut into wedges

1/2 lb smoked gouda, grated

1/2 cup cilantro, freshly chopped

Bamboo skewers, soaked in water

- Cut all the vegetables into equal medium sized pieces. Place the red onion and garlic onto the bamboo skewers.

- Drizzle the vegetables and skewers with oil and season with salt and pepper.

- Oil the grill and place the corn, skewers and veggies on the grill. Grill the corn for approximately 5 minutes turning often until tender.

- Continue to cook the vegetables and skewers for another 10 minutes or so until lightly charred and tender.

- Leave the grilled vegetables and corn to cool. Once cool, use a sharp knife to cut the corn from the cob. Place in a bowl. Cut the remaining vegetables into bite-sized pieces and add to the bowl.

- Add the grated cheese and cilantro.

- Remove the corn husks from the water and pat dry with paper towels.

- Place a healthy scoop of the vegetable mix into the middle of the husk. Close the husk over and tie the loose end so it sort of looks like a weird corn husk canoe filled with veggies.

- 10 minutes before serving, place the corn boats on the top rack of the barbecue at medium high heat. Close the lid. This will melt the cheese and heat the vegetables up again. Serve warm.

Serves 6

GRILLED VEGETABLES WITH GARLIC ANCHOVY DIP

This is our take on an old Italian favorite called "bagna cauda." This is an excellent sit-around-the-backyard-and-have-a-drink-and-a-few-laughs kind of starter to a Saturday night dinner party. The recipe calls for just one whole bulb of garlic but go ahead and add more if you don't plan on kissing anyone. You can also roast the garlic in the oven in advance to save time.

Dip

1 large bulb of garlic

Freshly ground cracked black pepper

3 sprigs of fresh thyme

1 tbsp of olive oil (15ml)

2 1/2 ounces of drained anchovy fillets, chopped (65g)

2 tbsp of unsalted butter, melted (30 ml)

1 cup of extra virgin olive oil (250ml)

Vegetables

3 red peppers

12 cherry tomatoes

6 small sweet potatoes (11/2 lbs)

6 carrots (375 g)

2 lbs of asparagus, trimmed (1000 g)

4 tbsp of extra virgin olive oil (60ml)

Salt and ground pepper to taste

Directions:

- Preheat the grill to medium-high heat.

- To make the dip first roast the garlic. Cut the top off of the garlic bulb. Using a fork, poke holes in the exposed garlic. Rub with olive oil and season with cracked black pepper. Add a few sprigs of thyme and wrap it all in tin foil. Place on the grill for approximately 1/2 hour.

- When the garlic has completely roasted, squish the bulbs from the skin into a blender. Add the chopped anchovies and butter and whiz. Season with freshly ground pepper.

- Pour the garlic anchovy mixture into the cup of olive oil. They should remain separated with the anchovy mixture sitting at the bottom of the oil.

- For the vegetables, cut the sweet potatoes, carrots, and red peppers lengthwise into large even pieces (thirds or quarters) and place them in a large glass bowl. Add the cherry tomatoes and asparagus. Add the olive oil and season generously. Toss the vegetables.

- Arrange the vegetables on the grill and cook for approximately 1 1/2 minutes per side with lid up.

- While the veggies are grilling, pour the dip into a pot and set on the grill to warm through. The aromas are insane.

- Serve warm with the dip on the side.

Serves 6

MARINATED CARROTS, PEARL ONIONS & RADISHES

Okay, so you don't actually barbecue this recipe. Marinated veggies as a starter with some nice cheese (like a brie or not-so-stinky Camembert) and good bread works great on a warm summer's night.

3/4 lb very young carrots, peeled and
*   trimmed (340g)*
1 cup pearl onions, skins removed (250ml)
1 cup radish, cleaned and stems
*   removed (250ml)*
3 cups water (750ml)
6 tbsp dry white wine (90ml)

Directions:

- In a medium size non-reactive saucepan, bring the water, wine, vinegar and olive oil to a boil with the garlic, parsley, thyme, oregano, sugar, salt, and cayenne.

- Reduce heat to medium and add the carrots, radish and onions. Cook for 5 minutes. Let cool in the saucepan.

6 tbsp white wine vinegar (90ml)

1/4 cup extra-virgin olive oil (60ml)

1 large garlic clove, crushed

1 small bunch fresh parsley

1 small bunch fresh thyme

1 small bunch fresh oregano

2 tbsp sugar (30ml)

1 tsp kosher salt

1 tsp cayenne pepper (5ml)

1 tsp Dijon mustard (5ml)

2 tbsp finely chopped fresh basil
    leaves (30ml)

- Pour the liquid and vegetables in a serving jar and refrigerate overnight.

- Next day, strain vegetables, reserving 2 cups of the poaching liquid. (500ml).

- Strain the liquid into a saucepan. Reduce over high heat to 1 cup (250ml). Stir in the mustard; cool.

- When ready to serve drizzle reduced sauce over vegetables and sprinkle with fresh chopped basil.

Makes 4 cups (1L) of vegetables servings

SMOKED CORN ON THE COB

The nice thing about corn is that it comes in its own grill container, namely the husk. Smoking adds a nice depth of flavor to the natural sugars in the corn. The bacon will melt and crisp up adding even more taste. Pretty easy, huh?

6 ears of corn with their husks, silks removed

Salt and pepper to taste

1 tbsp garlic powder (15ml)

1 tbsp cayenne pepper (15ml)

6 slices bacon

Wood chips for smoking

Directions:

- Pull back the husks of the corn keeping the base in tact. Remove all of the corn silk. Place the corn tip-down in a large stock pot of cold water to soak for an hour. You want to plump the corn up with water before smoking.

- Make a smoke pouch (see page 5).

- Prepare the barbecue for indirect grilling. Crank the heat on one side and place the first smoke pouch directly on the burner. Close the lid and wait for smoke. Once barbecue is smoking, reduce the heat to 220F/110C.

- Drain the corn and pat dry. Season each cob with salt and pepper, garlic powder and a pinch of cayenne.

- Wrap a slice of bacon around each cob. If necessary, use a water-soaked toothpick to secure the bacon to the cob.

- Pull the husks back over the cobs and place them on the unlit side of the grill.

- Close the lid and let the corn smoke for 1 hour.

Makes 6 cobs

GRILLED CORN WITH CHIPOTLE-MAPLE GLAZE

1/4 cup unsalted butter (60ml)

1/2 cup pure maple syrup (125ml)

1 tsp fresh minced garlic (5ml)

1 tsp onion salt (5ml)

1 tsp freshly ground black pepper (5ml)

1 tbsp minced canned chipotle chilies in
    adobo sauce (15ml)

6 ears fresh corn, husked

Directions:

- In a saucepan combine butter, maple syrup, garlic, onion salt, pepper and chipotle and bring to a simmer over low heat for 5 minutes, stirring occasionally.

- Place the corn on a baking sheet and brush with chipotle-maple glaze.

- Preheat the grill to medium heat.

- Oil the grill and add the corn. Grill for about 2 minutes.

- Baste and turn the corn to grill for a further 2 or 3 minutes.

- Remove from the grill and serve immediately.

Makes 6 cobs

ROASTED STUFFED PEARS

Barbecued pears for dessert? Smoked and stuffed and served with a very grown-up whipping cream on top. You can prep the pears in advance and store in the fridge until you need them. Just remember to take them out 30 minutes before smoking so they can return to room temperature.

6 firm-flesh Bartlett pears

5 tbsp unsalted butter, softened (75ml)

5 tbsp gingersnap cookies, crumbled (75ml)

2 tbsp brown sugar (30ml)

2 tsp chopped lemon zest (10ml)

1/2 tsp cinnamon (2.5ml)

1/4 tsp nutmeg (1ml)

Directions:

- In a bowl, combine room temperature butter and crumbled gingersnap cookies. Add brown sugar, lemon zest, cinnamon, nutmeg, cloves, orange liqueur, scraped vanilla seeds and mix.

- Slice a bit off of the bottom of each pear so that they stand up on a plate.

- Remove the tops and core each pear using a melonballer.

161

1/2 tsp ground cloves (2.5ml)

1 tbsp orange liqueur (15ml)

1 vanilla bean, scraped

1 lemon cut into wedges

Apple wood smoking chips

Whipping Cream

1 cup 35% cream (250ml)

Splash of orange liqueur

1/2 vanilla bean, scraped

1 tbsp icing sugar (15ml)

- *Tip – dampen a tea towel and place on countertop to hold the bowl in place while whipping*

- Rub the pears with lemon wedges to stop discoloring.

- Stuff the pears with the mixture – not too much – then put the tops back on.

- Butter a perforated barbecue baking sheet and add the pears.

- Make a smoke pouch (see page 5).

- Prepare the barbecue for indirect smoking. Crank the heat on one side and place the smoke pouch directly on the burner. Close the lid and wait for smoke. Once the barbecue is smoking, reduce the heat to 220F/110C.

- Place the pears on the unlit grill side. Close the lid and smoke the pears for approximately 30 minutes.

- Remove from heat and serve warm with this whipping cream:

Whipping Cream Directions:

- Place a large stainless steel bowl in the freezer and chill for 20 minutes.

- Take the cream out of the refrigerator and the bowl out of the freezer.

- Add a splash orange liqueur, vanilla seeds and icing sugar.

- Using a large balloon whisk, whip until soft peaks are achieved.

Serves 6 for dessert

SMOKED ACORN SQUASH WITH MAPLE SPICED BUTTER

They call it acorn squash because it sort of looks like a giant mutant acorn. Inside is a nice orange flesh that works incredibly well with the maple butter and the cranberries. Serve this as a side with chicken.

Maple Spiced Butter

3/4 cup unsalted butter, softened (185ml)

3 tbsp maple syrup (45ml)

1 tsp cinnamon (5ml)

1/2 tsp nutmeg (2.5ml)

Directions:

- Place all the Maple Spiced Butter ingredients into a small saucepan and simmer over low heat for 5 minutes.

- Brush inside cavity of the squash with 1/2 of the maple butter. Wrap the base of the squash in foil.

- Make a smoke pouch (see page 5).

Smoked Acorn Squash

3 acorn squash, cut in half, seeds and fibers
removed – about 1lb each (454g)
1 cup dried cranberries (250ml)
1/2 cup slivered almonds, toasted (125ml)

Apple or cherry wood chips.

- Prepare the barbecue for indirect smoking. Crank the heat on one side and place the smoke pouch directly on the burner. Close the lid and wait for smoke. Once the barbecue is smoking, reduce the heat to 220F/110C.

- Add acorn squash to unlit side, close the lid and smoke the squash for 1 hour or until soft and slightly caramelized (check for doneness with a fork).

- Remove from grill. Place acorn squash on a large serving platter. Cut the halves into thirds. Sprinkle with cranberries and toasted almonds.

- Top with a dollop of reserved room temperature maple butter.

Serves 6

GRILLED FENNEL WITH GARLIC ANCHOVY BUTTER

2 fennel bulbs

1 tbsp of extra virgin olive oil (15ml)

Garlic Anchovy Butter

5 tbsp butter, at room temperature (75 ml)

4 large garlic cloves

5 anchovy fillets

Juice from 1 lemon

1 tbsp of freshly chopped cilantro (15ml)

1 tsp of freshly ground black pepper (5ml)

Directions:

- Trim the fennel bulbs of their leafy tops.

- Cut the bulb into 3/4-inch wedges, being sure to leave the root end intact so that they don't fall apart on the grill.

- Preheat barbecue to medium high and oil the grill.

- Place the soft butter in a large bowl.

- Crush the garlic and add it to the bowl.

- Rinse the anchovy fillets and dice them. Add the diced anchovy, lemon juice, cilantro and pepper to the bowl and mix.

- Drizzle the fennel wedges with the olive oil. Grill the fennel for about 5 minutes a side with the lid up. Watch for flare ups and shift the vegetable if they persist.

- Serve hot with garlic anchovy butter melting on top.

Serves 4

GRILLED ANTIPASTO

Antipasto is Italian for "before the pasta" and refers to any sort of hors d'oeuvre which is French for "outside the work" and refers to small nibbles served before a meal. Kind of got a United Nations thing going on here, but all you need to know is this is a delicious way to start a dinner when everyone is sort of standing around in the backyard having a drink and listening to tunes. Got to love summer nights.

2/3 cup balsamic vinegar (150ml)

2 6-oz jar artichoke hearts (350ml)

*2 medium sweet red peppers sliced
   into 1-inch pieces*

*2 medium sweet yellow peppers sliced
   into 1-inch pieces*

*16 small whole or 8 medium halved cipollini
   or 16 pearl onions*

16 large crimini or button mushrooms caps

*4 ounces of feta cheese sliced into thin,
   short strips (125ml)*

1/4 cup black olives (60ml)

1/3 cup fresh parsley (75ml)

1/3 cup fresh basil (75 ml)

Salt and pepper - to taste

8 long metal skewers

Directions:

- In a saucepan, bring the balsamic vinegar to boil. Let simmer for 5 minutes uncovered or until the vinegar reduced to 6 tbsp (90ml), and set aside to cool.

- Drain the artichokes, reserving 4 tbsp (60ml) of artichoke juice and set aside.

- Skewer the red and yellow peppers, cipollini and mushroom, leaving a 1/4-inch space between each vegetable.

- In a small bowl, combine the reserved balsamic vinegar with the artichoke juice. Brush half of the vinegar mixture evenly over the vegetable skewers.

- Preheat the barbecue to medium, oil the grill.

- Grill the skewers directly over the heat with lid closed for 4–5 minutes or until vegetables are tender.

- Turn once, brushing with the remaining vinegar mixture. Continue grilling for another 4–5 minutes.

- Once vegetables are grilled, remove from the skewers and place in a large salad bowl.

- Add drained artichoke, cheese, black olives, basil, parsley and season with salt and pepper, toss gently to combine all ingredients.

- Serve on crackers, grilled bread or endive spears

Serves 10–12

GRILLED ASPARAGUS AND BEETS

Beets come in all sorts of colors and sizes. Go for the ones a bit smaller than the size of a tennis ball. The asparagus should be about as think as your pinky. Make sure you put on rubber gloves to slice the beets or you'll end up with red hands.

2 lbs summer beets, mixed colors (1kg)

2 lbs asparagus

2 tbsp olive oil (30ml)

1 tbsp balsamic vinegar (15ml)

Salt and pepper to taste

1/4 cup fresh basil, chopped roughly (60ml)

Directions:

- Add summer beets to a pot of boiling water and cook for about 7 minutes or until the beets are tender. The exact time will vary depending on how big your beets are. You should be able to poke a fork through to the middle.

- Drain the beets under cold running water.

- Skin the beets, then slice them 1/3-inch thick and place them on a baking sheet.

- Next, snap the woody ends off the asparagus and place them on the baking sheet with the beets.

- Drizzle the asparagus and beets with oil, balsamic vinegar, salt and pepper.

- Preheat the barbecue to high heat and oil the grill

- Grill the beet slices for about 2 minutes

- Flip the beets and add the asparagus. Grill for another 2 minutes

- Remove from the grill and serve right away, topped with the basil

Serves 6–8

GRILLED HONEY-TARRAGON CARROTS

Tarragon is an underused herb with sort of a lemony-licorice kick to it. It goes so well with honey, which goes so well with carrots. Don't use the big honkin' telephone pole carrots, instead go for ones about as thick as your thumb. This side goes nicely with chicken, pork tenderloin or some grilled fish.

14 fresh carrots

3 tbsp sesame oil (45ml)

3 tbsp honey (45ml)

3 tsp chopped ginger (45ml)

4 tarragon sprigs, torn

3 tbsp vegetable oil (45ml)

Salt and pepper to taste

Directions:

- Cut the leafy tops off the carrots leaving only half an inch at the root.

- Wash and peel the carrots and cut them in half lengthwise.

- Put them into a sealable plastic bag and drizzle with sesame oil, honey, ginger and tarragon.

- Toss to coat and marinate at room temperature for about 30 minutes.

- Preheat the barbecue to medium heat.

- Oil the grill. Place carrots flat-side down over direct heat and cook for 3 minutes or so depending on how thick the carrots are.

- Flip and continue grilling for a minute or two.

- Remove from the heat and serve warm.

Serves 7

Salad

Asian Flavored Coleslaw

Baby Arugula Salad with Pine Nuts, Cranberries & Dressing

Big Man Caesar Salad

Chicory Chorizo Salad

Avocado, Grapefruit, Red Onion & Feta Salad

Corn, Red Pepper & Arugula Salad

Fennel & Orange Salad

Tomato & Grilled Bread Salad

Summer Potato Salad

Banana & Spud Salad

Cabbage Salad

Carrot Salad

Green Bean Salad

Wild Rice Pecan Salad

Pasta Salad with Grilled Corn & Jalapenos

Couscous Salad with Grilled Vegetables

Watermelon Salad

ASIAN FLAVORED COLESLAW

What *doesn't* coleslaw go with? Okay, maybe French Toast…and birthday cake…it would probably suck with birthday cake. But it goes with pretty much anything that comes off the barbecue. We throw an Asian curve by including sesame seeds, ginger, sesame oil, and rice vinegar. Try this next to a sandwich and some fries.

1 tsp sesame seeds (5ml)

4 cups (1L) thinly sliced Napa cabbage
(about 1/2 large head)

1/2 red pepper, thinly sliced

1/2 yellow pepper, thinly sliced

1/2 cup thinly sliced green onions (125ml)

Asian Dressing

3 tbsp rice vinegar (50ml)

2 tbsp peanut oil (30ml)

1 tbsp minced fresh ginger (15ml)

1 tsp sesame oil (5ml)

1 tsp sugar (5ml)

2 tsp Asian hot sauce (10ml)

Directions:

- Stir sesame seeds in a dry non-stick skillet over medium heat until golden (about 3 minutes), then set aside

- Combine cabbage, red and yellow peppers and green onions in a large bowl.

- In a separate bowl mix together dressing ingredients to combine. Toss with cabbage mixture and season to taste with salt and pepper.

- Sprinkle with seeds and serve

Serves 6

BABY ARUGULA SALAD WITH PINE NUTS, CRANBERRIES AND DRESSING

Arugula is far and away my most favorite salad green. I could eat it every night. The baby leaves are more tender than the grown-up variety (kind of like people, really). Arugula has a nice sort of peppery taste, so Parmesan (salty) and peaches (sweet) go really well with this salad green.

Salad

3 tbsp pine nuts (45ml)

4 cups organic baby arugula (500g or 1 litre)

2 fresh peaches cut into 1/4-inch thick wedges

1/2 cup coarsely shredded Parmesan cheese
   (125ml)

Dressing

4 tbsp olive oil (60ml)

3 tbsp raspberry vinegar (45ml)

Juice of 1 lime

1 shallot, diced

Salt and pepper to taste

Pinch of sugar to taste

Directions:

- Place pine nuts in a non-stick skillet and roast over low heat until golden brown.

- Divide the baby arugula between four salad plates. Top with peach wedges and roasted pine nuts and sprinkle with shredded Parmesan.

- In a separate bowl, combine olive oil, raspberry vinegar, lime juice, diced shallot and salt and pepper. Whisk ingredients together. Taste and adjust acidity with sugar.

- Drizzle dressing over salads and serve. Not too much dressing! You don't want to drown out the other flavors on the plate.

Serves 4

BIG MAN CAESAR SALAD

I swear there are more ways to make a Caesar than just about any other salad. Some people like to add the Parmesan to the dressing, others like it on top. If you're going to make this salad on a regular basis then it's worth investing in a wooden bowl that you don't use for anything else, because after a while the garlic will permeate the wood of the bowl and affect the taste of anything else you put in there.

Caesar Salad Dressing

2 cloves garlic

Salt and cracked black pepper

2 tsp Dijon or dry mustard (10ml)

2 egg yolks

4 tsp of anchovy paste (20ml)

2 lemons, juiced

2 tbsp Worcestershire sauce (30ml)

1 cup olive oil (250ml)

2 romaine lettuces heads

5 slices bacon, cooked to crispy

1/4 cup shaved Parmesan cheese (62ml)

1 cup croutons (250ml)

Directions:

- Crush the garlic cloves in a wooden salad bowl and add a pinch of salt.

- Add the cracked pepper, mustard, egg yolks, anchovy paste, lemon juice and Worcestershire sauce. Stir vigorously.

- Add the olive oil in a steady stream and stir until emulsified. Add salt to taste.

- Shred the cleaned romaine lettuce leaves and add to the salad bowl. Mix until salad is well coated with the dressing.

- Top with bacon, Parmesan and croutons.

- Serve and enjoy!

Serves 6–8

CHICORY CHORIZO SALAD

Chorizo is a Spanish pork sausage heavy on the garlic, paprika and spices. Very delicious. Chicory is a peppery and bitter green. Also delicious. Asiago is a semi-soft Italian cheese with a nice nutty taste. Mucho delicious. Put them all together in a bowl with some tomatoes and roast garlic dressing and BOOM, you've got yourself an amazing salad.

1/2-lb chorizo sausage

4 cups chicory, washed and cleaned (1 liter)

1/2 cup cilantro, chopped (125ml)

2 medium tomatoes cut into eighths

1 cup roasted garlic vinaigrette (250ml),
*   store bought*

1/4-lb Asiago cheese, finely shaved

Directions:

- Grill the sausage in a skillet over medium-low heat for 10 minutes to render fat.

- Remove from pan, drain on paper towels. Slice into thin discs and set aside.

- Place chopped chicory and cilantro into large bowl, add tomatoes and toss.

- Add Asiago cheese and cooled sausage.

- Drizzle the roasted garlic vinaigrette on the salad just before serving.

Serves 4

AVOCADO, GRAPEFRUIT, RED ONION AND FETA SALAD

I love a salad now and then that isn't just all greens with a bit of dressing. Peppery arugula, creamy avocado, tart grapefruit, salty feta and nippy onion make for a nice change with a great piece of fish and some good, crisp white wine.

2 large bunches arugula, washed and trimmed

2 large avocados, halved, pit removed,
  peeled, sliced lengthwise

1 large red or pink grapefruit, peeled and
  sectioned, any juice reserved

1 medium size red onion, thinly sliced

3 oz feta cheese, crumbled (about 1/2 cup)

1/2 cup best-quality plain yogurt (125ml)

3 tbsp honey (45ml)

1/3 cup fresh orange juice (83ml)

Salt and freshly ground black pepper to taste

Directions:

- In a bowl gently toss the arugula, avocado, grapefruit, onions and feta cheese.

- In a separate bowl combine yogurt, honey, grapefruit juice, orange juice, salt and pepper.

- Just before serving, spoon some of this dressing over the salad and toss until well coated.

Serves 6

CORN, RED PEPPER AND ARUGULA SALAD

I'm a nut for arugula. Come summertime you can get the baby variety in most decent green grocers. If you go for the grown-up arugula, just remove the spines from some of the bigger leaves.

3 ears of corn, husks and silks removed

2 red bell peppers

1 yellow bell pepper

6 tbsp extra-virgin olive oil (90 ml)

4 cups arugula, washed and dried

1/2 cup sliced red onion (125 ml)

1/2 cup feta cheese, crumbled (125 ml)

2 tbsp balsamic vinegar (30ml)

Salt and pepper to taste

Directions:

- Crank barbecue to medium high and oil the grill.

- Drizzle the corn and peppers with 2 tbsp (30ml) of olive oil.

- Place the peppers on grill and cook for 7–8 minutes, turning every now and then, until peppers are charred and blistered. Remove and let cool.

- Place corn on grill for 4–5 minutes. Rotate the corn when the color turns vibrant yellow and slightly charred. Remove and let cool.

- Peel the skins and remove the seeds from the peppers and roughly dice (the pepper, not the seeds). Place the peppers in a large bowl. Strip the kernels from cobs and add to bowl.

- Add the arugula, red onion and feta.

- Before serving, drizzle balsamic vinegar and remaining olive oil over the salad and toss.

Serves 6

FENNEL & ORANGE SALAD

Fennel has a very mild sort of licorice flavor to it which plays off nicely against the sweet orange and peppery watercress in this salad. Normally I say load on the garlic but don't go too crazy here or you'll drown out the other flavors.

Dressing

1/2 cup fresh orange juice (125ml)

2/3 cup olive oil (150ml)

Splash of hot sauce

4 cloves garlic, minced

4 tbsp fresh flat leaf parsley, chopped (60ml)

Salt and pepper to taste

3 fennel bulbs, thinly sliced with core intact

3 oranges

1 large bunch of watercress, tough stems removed

1/2 cup honey-roasted macadamia nuts (125ml)

Directions:

- In a glass bowl, mix the dressing ingredients.

- Place thinly sliced fennel in a sealable plastic bag or a ceramic dish. Pour two-thirds of the dressing over the fennel and set the rest of the dressing aside. Seal the bag and place in the fridge for at least 5 hours. Remove from the fridge a good 30 minutes before grilling.

- Using a knife, trim the skin off of the oranges and segment the slices.

- Preheat the grill to medium high. Oil the grill and cook the fennel, lid up, for 3 minutes per side (depending on how thick you sliced it).

- Add orange slices to grill for last minute of grilling.

- Toss grilled fennel and orange with the watercress and honey-roasted macadamia nuts. Drizzle with the reserved marinade and serve while still warm.

Serves 6

TOMATO & GRILLED BREAD SALAD

This salad has been around probably as long as bread has. You can leave out the jalapeno and load up on the basil if you prefer.

3 1-inch thick slices of French bread

2 tbsp olive oil (30ml)

4 large vine-ripened tomatoes, cut in wedges

1/2 red onion, sliced thin

1 small jalapeno pepper, diced

2 cloves garlic

1/2 cup chopped chives (125ml)

3 tbsp basil, leaves torn (45ml)

1/4 cup balsamic vinegar (62ml)

1 tsp salt and pepper (5ml)

Directions:

- Preheat the grill to medium high.

- Rub olive oil on both sides of the sliced bread.

- Oil the grill and toast the bread until very crisp. Leave the slices to cool then cut them into 1 inch squares.

- Combine the remaining ingredients in a bowl and toss gently. Add bread cubes and toss again. Cover and let sit for 10 minutes before serving.

Serves 4

SUMMER POTATO SALAD

Hey, what's barbecue without potato salad, right? There's a whole lot of flavors and textures going on in this one with the cilantro, olives, celery and gherkins.

2 lbs small red or white new potatoes,
    scrubbed (907g)

1/3 cup fresh chopped parsley (80ml)

1/4 cup fresh chopped cilantro (60ml)

2 cups canned or jarred artichoke hearts,
    drained and quartered (500ml)

1 cup black kalamata olives, pitted (250ml)

2 large ribs celery, diced small

4 small gherkins, chopped fine

3 cloves garlic, minced

1/4 cup fresh lemon juice (60ml)

1 tsp salt (5ml)

1 tsp fresh black pepper (5ml)

1 tsp cumin (5ml)

1/2 tsp cayenne pepper (2.5ml)

1 tsp sugar (5ml)

1/2 tsp paprika (2.5ml)

1/2 cup olive oil (125ml)

Additional salt and pepper to taste

Directions:

- Place potatoes in a large uncovered pot of boiling salted water. Let potatoes boil for 5–7 minutes.

- Strain potatoes in a colander and run under cold water to stop the cooking process.

- When the potatoes are cooled, slice each in half. Place in a large bowl.

- Combine the potatoes with the parsley, cilantro, artichoke hearts, olives, chopped gherkins and celery ribs.

- Place garlic in a food processor and puree. Add the lemon juice, salt, pepper, cumin, cayenne, paprika and sugar. Blitz and slowly add the olive oil, processing until the dressing is thickened and emulsified.

- Mix the dressing with the salad and refrigerate for 30 minutes to infuse flavors.

- Add salt and pepper to taste.

Serves 6–8

BANANA AND SPUD SALAD

No we're not crazy. Okay, we are crazy *but* bananas and spuds really work in this off-the-wall play on the traditional potato salad. Make sure the bananas are a bit green so they hold up to the boiling water you're going to dunk them in.

2 lbs red or white baby potatoes (1kg)

1 1/2 lbs greenish bananas (4 or 5)

1 red onion, sliced thin

1 red bell pepper, sliced thin

1/4 cup capers, drained (60ml)

4 tbsp olive oil (60ml)

2 tbsp white wine vinegar (30ml)

1 tbsp Dijon mustard (15ml)

2 1/2 tsp salt (12.5ml)

1 tsp cracked black pepper (5ml)

3 tbsp chives (15ml)

Directions:

- Wash the potatoes with the skins on.

- Place the spuds in a pot of boiling water for 7 minutes, or until just cooked.

- Drain and run under cool water in a colander to stop the cooking process.

- Cool and cut into halves

- Bring another pot of water to a boil.

- Working quickly, peel bananas and begin slicing into boiling water to cook for just 30 seconds.

- Once cooked, drain the bananas in a colander.

- Place potatoes and bananas into bowl and add sliced onion, red pepper and capers.

- In a separate bowl whisk together olive oil vinegar, mustard, salt, pepper and chives. Pour over top and toss.

- Into the refrigerator to cool.

Serves 6–8

CABBAGE SALAD

1/2 head green cabbage, grated or sliced thin

1/2 head red cabbage, grated or slice thin

3 carrots cut into matchsticks

1 red pepper, sliced into strips

2 jalapeno, chopped

4 green onions, chopped

Dressing

1 cup sour cream (250ml)

3 tbsp mayonnaise (45ml)

2 tbsp apple cider vinegar (45ml)

2 tbsp smoked chipotle pepper,
    chopped (45ml)

1 tsp celery salt (5ml)

2 tbsp molasses (30ml)

Directions:

- Mix all ingredients for dressing in a large bowl.

- Add the fresh vegetables and toss.

- Place in the refrigerator for at least 2 hours for flavors to blend.

Serves 6

CARROT SALAD

Another way of doing this is to slice the carrots lengthwise and grill them 'til nicely charred, then toss with the dressing and serve as a side dish with salmon or chicken.

6 carrots, peeled, cut on a 1/4-inch bias

1 tbsp olive oil (15ml)

Salt and pepper to taste

1 cup sliced snow peas (250ml)

1 cup green pea shoots or salad greens (250ml)

Bamboo skewers soaked in water for 1 hour

Dressing

Juice of 2 oranges

Juice of 1 lime

1 tsp honey (5ml)

1 tsp chopped ginger (5ml)

1 tsp sugar (5ml)

Pinch of salt

Pinch of pepper

2 tbsp olive oil (30ml)

Directions:

- To prepare dressing, whisk together all ingredients in a medium sized bowl.

- Preheat the barbecue to medium high.

- Skewer the carrot strips onto soaked bamboo skewers.

- Place skewered carrots on grill for 1–2 minutes per side or until lightly charred.

- Remove carrots from grill and toss into a large salad bowl with snow peas, greens and salad dressing.

- Serve immediately.

Serves 4

GREEN BEAN SALAD

You can either serve this on its own as a starter or as a side dish with chicken or pork.

1 lb green beans (450 g)

3 cloves garlic

1/4 cup extra virgin olive oil (60ml)

2 tsp honey (10ml)

2 tbsp red wine vinegar (30ml)

1/2 cup hazelnuts, crushed (125ml)

1 cup shallots, thinly sliced (250ml)

1/2 cup pitted kalamata olives (125ml)

1 tsp salt (5ml)

1/2 tsp black pepper, freshly ground (2.5ml)

Directions:

- Bring water to a boil in a large pot, add the beans and cook for 2 minutes. Immediately strain and plunge the beans into a bowl full of ice water to stop the cooking process.

- Fine dice the garlic and add to a small bowl. Using a whisk add olive oil, honey and red wine vinegar.

- Pour mixture over beans add nuts, shallots, olives, and salt and pepper to taste.

- Toss and chill well before serving.

Serves 4

WILD RICE PECAN SALAD

Wild rice isn't actually a rice (it's a grain) and it has a nice bite and a great nutty flavor. Combined with the 'shrooms and cranberries this is a great side dish for steak or lamb or pork.

1 1/2 cups uncooked wild rice (375ml)

6 ounces wild mushrooms, cut into small
   thin slices

1/2 cup dried cranberries (125 ml)

3 green onions, minced

Zest of 1 orange

Dressing

2 tbsp olive oil (30ml)

Juice of 1 orange

1/2 tsp prepared horseradish (2.5ml)

Salt to season

1/2 cup pecan pieces toasted (125ml)

Directions:

- Cook the wild rice according the package instructions and pour the finished rice into a bowl to cool to room temperature.

- Add mushrooms, cranberries, green onion and orange zest.

- Whisk the ingredients for the dressing together in another bowl. Pour the dressing over the salad and mix it well.

- Cover the salad with plastic wrap and refrigerate for 1 hour to 24 hours.

- Place pecans on a tray and place on grill to toast.

- Stir the pecans into the salad and serve chilled.

Serves 6

PASTA SALAD WITH GRILLED CORN & JALAPENOS

For some reason, revenge and pasta salad are two dishes best served cold. *Al dente* is
Italian for "to the tooth" and means cooking the pasta 'til it has a bit of resistance
when you bite into it, maybe 2 minutes less than you normally would (depending on
the pasta). There are a lot of steps here but it's a pretty easy recipe.

11 oz short pasta such as penne (453g)

4 ears fresh corn, shucked and silks removed

4 jalapeno chili peppers

1 large white onion, cut in 1/2-inch-thick rounds

Olive oil for drizzling

8 medium tomatoes

3 tbsp chopped fresh basil (45ml)

Directions:

- Lay corn, jalapenos and onion on baking sheet.
  Drizzle vegetables with olive oil.

- Preheat the barbecue to medium-high heat on one
  side and medium-low heat on the other.

- Oil the grill and add the onions to the medium-low
  side first, then add the corn and jalapenos to the
  medium-high heat side.

3 tbsp chopped fresh oregano (45ml)

3 tbsp chopped fresh cilantro (45ml)

1/3 cup green (hulled) pumpkin seeds (80ml)

1/4 cup olive oil (6oml)

4 cloves garlic, minced

1 tsp ground cumin (5ml)

Salt and pepper to taste

1 1/2 cups crumbled feta cheese (250 ml)

Garnish: fresh cilantro leaves

- Grill the onions to char, about 5 minutes.

- Grill the corn and jalapenos to char for about 2–3 minutes, turning to prevent burning.

- Remove the vegetables from grill and let cool to room temperature.

- Remove skins and seeds from jalapenos and place cleaned peppers into a bowl.

- Cut the corn off the cob and into the bowl.

- Chop the onion and quarter the tomatoes and then into the bowl.

- Add basil, oregano and cilantro.

- Meanwhile, cook pasta in a pot of boiling water, following instructions for al dente. Once cooked, place in colander to rinse under cold water. Shake off excess water and add to bowl. Drizzle with some olive oil.

- Next, in a non-stick skillet, toast the pumpkin seeds over low heat until lightly browned. Add to salad ingredients in bowl.

- In another non-stick skillet heat oil, add garlic and cumin. Cook for 3 minutes stirring with wooden spoon over medium-low heat. Add the flavored oil to the salad, toss, season with salt and pepper, refrigerate.

Serves 6–8

COUSCOUS SALAD WITH GRILLED VEGETABLES

Couscous looks like a little grain but is really granular semolina. A staple of North African cuisine, couscous cooks in no time and absorbs the flavor of whatever you add to it. It's a great, quick alternative when the family is tired of pasta. For added flavor use chicken or veggie stock instead of water for the couscous.

1 red onion cut into 3-inch wedges

2 medium zucchini, each cut lengthwise into 4 wedges

3 large leeks, (white and pale green parts only) quartered lengthwise

1 red bell pepper, cut into 3-inch strips

1/4 cup plus 4 tbsp of olive oil

2 1/2 cups water

1 tsp salt

1 10-oz box of couscous

3 tbsp balsamic vinegar

2 tbsp chopped fresh thyme

2 tbsp chopped fresh rosemary

2 tbsp chopped fresh oregano

4 tbsp thinly sliced fresh basil

6 tbsp fresh lemon juice

1 cup pitted and halved kalamata olives

4 tbsp drained capers

Directions:

- Preheat grill to medium high.

- Cut all of the vegetables into roughly the same size and place on a large platter. Drizzle with 4 tbsp of olive oil and ensure that everything is well coated.

- Season the vegetables generously with salt and pepper.

- Oil the grill and add the vegetable wedges. Grill for about 2–4 minutes per side, or until cooked through with nice grill marks. Remove and cool.

- In a large pot, bring the water to a boil. Place the dry couscous in a large bowl. Pour the boiling water overtop and cover in plastic wrap. Leave to sit for 5 minutes.

- Meanwhile, chop the grilled vegetables up into bite-sized pieces. When the couscous is ready, stir to fluff it up and mix in the vegetables.

- Add the remaining olive oil, herbs, lemon juice, olives and capers and mix.

- Cover again with plastic wrap and let sit at room temperature until ready to serve.

Serves 6

WATERMELON SALAD

With the vodka and Grand Marnier this is obviously a very grown-up salad. I like to use this as a palate cleanser between courses instead of as a salad at the beginning of the meal. It's light and refreshing and the booze will have your guests dancing on the table. Just keep them away from the pool.

1 8-lb seedless watermelon, (3.6 kg or
   about 16 cups, cubed)

1/2 cup fresh lemon juice (125 ml)

1/2 cup fresh lime juice (125 ml)

2/3 cup sugar (150 ml)

1/2 cup vodka (125 ml)

6 tbsp Grand Marnier (90 ml)

1/4 cup chopped fresh mint (60 ml)

Directions:

- Cut the watermelon out of rind and cube it into 1-inch pieces. Put all watermelon into a big bowl.

- In a separate bowl, squeeze the lemons and limes. Add sugar and stir until it is dissolved.

- Add the vodka and Grand Marnier.

- Pour mixture over the watermelon and add fresh mint; stir gently to combine.

- Put the salad in the refrigerator for an hour to set up. Don't leave it any longer than that or the watermelon will get all mooshy.

Serves 8

Sauces

Homemade Smoked Ketchup

Golden Mustard Barbecue Sauce

Hot Chili Barbecue Sauce

Maple Mango Barbecue Sauce

Tomatillo Salsa

Banana Salsa

Plum Chutney

Lemon Honey Sauce with Garlic

Sweet & Spicy Mint Sauce

Passion Fruit Applesauce

Pernod Butter

Sweet & Sour Barbecue Sauce

HOMEMADE SMOKED KETCHUP

Hey, why buy ketchup when you can make your own? We snuck into the Heinz plant under cover of night and stole their secret recipe. Kidding. Smoking the tomatoes with hickory wood chips ensures that this tastes nothing like any ketchup you've ever had before. Ketchup or catsup (depending on where you're from) has been around for at least 300 years and is said to have originated in China. Seriously. This time I'm not kidding.

2 lbs tomatoes, halved and seeded

3 tbsp olive oil (45ml)

1 tbsp white sugar (15ml)

garlic cloves, peeled (one for each
*   tomato half)*

1/2 cup sweet onion, finely diced (125 ml)

3 tbsp cider vinegar (45ml)

2 tbsp brown sugar (30ml)

1 tsp ground allspice (5ml)

1/2 tsp ground cumin (2.5ml)

1/4 tsp ground nutmeg (1.25 ml)

1 tsp Worcestershire sauce (5ml)

Hickory wood chips for smoking

Directions:

- Make a smoke pouch (see page 5).

- Place the tomatoes on a perforated barbecue baking sheet and drizzle with 1 tbsp of oil until well coated. Sprinkle with sugar.

- Place a garlic clove into each of the tomato halves.

- Prepare the barbecue for indirect grilling. Crank the heat on one side and place the smoke pouch directly on the burner. Close the lid and wait for smoke. Once barbecue is smoking, reduce the heat to 220F/110C.

- Place the tomatoes on the side of the barbecue where there is no direct heat. Close the lid and smoke the tomatoes for 1 1/4 hours.

- Once fully smoked, put the tomatoes and garlic in a blender and blitz.

- In a saucepan set over medium heat, sauté the onions in oil until tender but not browned.

- Add the pureed tomato and garlic to the saucepan.

- Add vinegar, brown sugar, allspice, cumin, nutmeg and Worcestershire sauce.

- Simmer over medium heat for 30 minutes until thickened.

- Season to taste and leave to cool.

- This will keep for up to 1 week covered in fridge.

GOLDEN MUSTARD BARBECUE SAUCE

1 cup white vinegar (250ml)

1/2 cup prepared yellow mustard (125ml)

1/4 cup Dijon mustard (60ml)

1/2 medium onion, minced

1/3 cup water (83ml)

1/4 cup tomato paste (60ml)

1 tbsp paprika (15ml)

2 tbsp brown sugar (30ml)

7 cloves garlic, minced

2 tsp celery salt (10ml)

1/2 tsp cayenne (2.5ml)

1/2 tsp freshly ground black pepper (2.5ml)

Directions:

- Place all of the ingredients into a non-reactive heavy bottomed saucepan over medium-high heat and bring to a simmer.

- Reduce heat to low and cook for 25 minutes, simmering until the mixture thickens and the onions are tender. Serve warm or cold.

- This will keep for 2 weeks covered in the refrigerator.

Yield: 2 1/2 cups (625ml)

HOT CHILI BARBECUE SAUCE

This recipe calls for four different types of chili peppers. Not only do different peppers have different heat quotients, they also have different tastes. Combining them brings depth of flavor to your sauce and every Barbecue Master (or Mistress) is known for his hot barbecue sauce, so don't mess around. Try and use at least 3 of them if you can't find all four. If your local grocer doesn't have chipotles, it's time to get a new grocer.

1 small poblano pepper, seeded and diced

1 serrano chili, seeded and finely diced

1 Thai chili, finely diced

1 tbsp olive oil (15ml)

*2 canned chipotle peppers in adobo
    sauce, minced*

1 small white onion, diced fine

1 tbsp minced garlic (15ml)

1 cup tomato sauce (250ml)

1/4 cup ketchup (60ml)

2 tbsp prepared mustard (30ml)

2 tbsp prepared horseradish (30ml)

1 1/2 tsp ground cinnamon (7.5ml)

3 tbsp molasses (45ml)

1 tbsp Worcestershire sauce (15ml)

1/2 tsp soy sauce (7.5ml)

Salt and pepper to taste

Directions:

- In large skillet heat the oil over medium heat until almost smoking, add the fresh chilies and cook for 2 minutes or until slightly charred.

- Add garlic and onion and sauté until translucent.

- Add the remaining ingredients and bring to a simmer.

- Reduce heat to low and simmer for 30 minutes. Adjust seasoning if necessary.

Yield: 2 cups (500ml)

MAPLE MANGO BARBECUE SAUCE

Maple mango barbecue sauce. Try saying that three times fast. This one is fast and easy and is perfect with pork or chicken.

1/2 cup maple syrup (125ml)

1/2 cup mango chutney (125ml)

1/2 cup ketchup (125ml)

1/2 cup bottled barbecue sauce (125ml)

1/2 cup tomato sauce (125ml)

1 tbsp ginger powder (15ml)

1 tbsp onion powder (15ml)

1 tbsp celery salt (15ml)

1 tbsp lemon pepper (15ml)

2 tbsp hot sauce (optional) (30ml)

Juice of 1 lemon

Directions:

- Place all of the ingredients into a non-reactive heavy-bottomed saucepan. Place over medium-low heat and cook for 20 minutes without letting the sauce boil. Stir occasionally.

Yield: 2 1/2 cups (625 ml)

TOMATILLO SALSA

Tomatillos are also known in some places as Mexican green tomatoes and are not tomatoes at all but rather are related to the gooseberry. Most times you're going to get them when they're green which is a good thing for this salsa because they'll be nice and firm. Tomatillos have a sort of lemony apple flavor (that's not quite it, but it's the closest I can come up with) that makes for a great salsa when combined with the chili, cilantro and red pepper. Nice colors too. Works really well with a big meaty fish or a nice veal chop.

8 tomatillos, husks discarded

2 fresh jalapeno chilies with seeds, chopped

1 cup fresh cilantro leaves, washed well
   and spun dry (250ml)

1/4 cup water (60ml)

1 tsp coarse salt (5ml)

2 shallots diced fine

1 medium sweet red pepper, diced fine

Directions:

- Rinse tomatillos under warm water to remove sticky film and pat dry with paper towel.

- Quarter the tomatillos and place in a blender with the jalapeno, cilantro and water.

- Puree in bursts until chunky.

- Pour mixture into a bowl and add salt, diced shallot and red pepper.

- Cover and let rest in fridge.

- Bring salsa to room temperature before serving.

Yield: 1 cup (250ml)

BANANA SALSA

You are going to love this with chicken or red snapper. The chipotles give the salsa some heat and smokiness.

4 ripe bananas, peeled and diced
   (about 2 cups) (500ml)

2 chipotle peppers from a can, finely diced

1/2 medium red pepper, finely diced

1/2 cup finely diced red onion, (125ml)

4 tbsp freshly chopped mint (60ml)

2 tbsp orange juice (30ml)

2 tbsp freshly squeezed lime juice (30ml)

1 tbsp honey (15ml)

Directions:

- Combine all of the ingredients except the banana into a bowl. Toss gently. Add the banana and toss again to coat. Cover and place in the refrigerator for 2–3 hours.

Yield: 3 cups (750ml)

PLUM CHUTNEY

1 lb red plums, ripe but still firm

1 large Gala apple

2/3 cup sugar (225ml)

1 cup water (250 ml)

6 tbsp red wine vinegar (90ml)

1 tbsp peeled and minced fresh ginger (15ml)

1 tsp chopped garlic (5ml)

2 tsp grated orange zest (30ml)

2 tsp nutmeg (10ml)

2 tsp cloves (10ml)

1 tsp cinnamon (5 ml)

Directions:

- Halve and pit the plums. Dice into 1/2-inch cubes and place in a bowl.

- Core and halve the apples leaving the skins on. Dice into 1/2-inch cubes.

- In a saucepan, dissolve the sugar in the water and bring to a gentle boil over medium-high heat.

- Add vinegar, ginger, garlic, diced apples and half of the diced plums.

- Bring mixture to a gentle boil and simmer for 5 minutes.

- Add the remaining plums, orange zest, nutmeg, cloves and cinnamon.

- Bring to a gentle boil and cook for 10 minutes or until thick and syrupy

- Remove and cool.

- Serve at room temperature.

Yield: 2 cups (500ml)

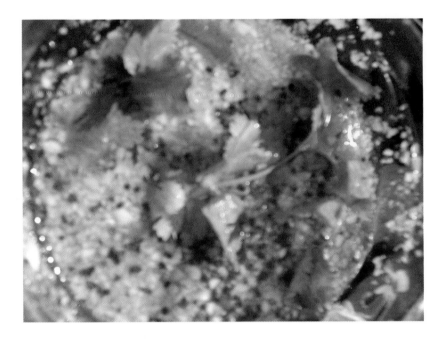

LEMON HONEY SAUCE WITH GARLIC

FIFTEEN CLOVES OF GARLIC!! Trust me, this works. Adjust the number of chilies to suit your heat tolerance.

15 cloves of garlic, minced

1 hot chili, seeded and finely chopped

4 tbsp minced fresh cilantro (60ml)

Juice of 2 lemons

8 tbsp honey (120ml)

1 tsp fish sauce (5ml)

Directions:

- Combine all of the ingredients in a bowl and whisk until fully incorporated. Adjust seasoning as desired and serve immediately.

Yield: 1 1/2 cups (375ml)

SWEET & SPICY MINT SAUCE

The trick is to make it *look* like you spent forever making dinner. This sauce is great with lamb or shrimp.

3/4 cup mint jelly (187ml)

1/2 cup white vinegar (125ml)

1 red Thai chili, split, seeded and finely diced

1/4 cup chopped fresh mint

Directions:

- Combine all of the ingredients in a saucepan and bring to a boil.

- Reduce heat slightly and simmer for 3 minutes and serve immediately.

- If the sauce becomes too thick, add a tsp of water at a time until you reach desired consistency.

- Add chopped fresh mint prior to serving.

Yield: 1 1/4 cup (310ml)

PASSION FRUIT APPLESAUCE

2 1/2 cups of applesauce (600ml)

1 cup strained passion fruit sauce,
    pulp or nectar (250ml)

1 tsp vanilla extract (5ml)

3 slices peeled and minced fresh ginger
    (1/4 inch think)

1/4 cup dark Jamaican rum (60ml)

3 tbsp honey (or more to taste) (45ml)

1 cinnamon stick

1 tsp allspice (5ml)

Directions:

- Combine all of the ingredients in a heavy-bottomed saucepan and bring to a boil.

- Lower the heat and simmer for 15 minutes.

Yield: About 4 cups (1L)

PERNOD BUTTER

Pernod is a French licorice-flavored liqueur and makes for a great compound butter to be served with fish or shellfish.

1/4-lb unsalted butter, softened

3 tbsp Pernod (45ml)

1 tsp pepper

Directions:

- Mix all of the ingredients together in a bowl.

- Scrape the butter into a piece of plastic wrap and roll into a log shape.

- Place in the fridge to set.

Yield: 1/4 lb of butter (450g)

SWEET & SOUR BARBECUE SAUCE

1/2 cup bottled plum sauce (125ml)

3 tbsp soy sauce (45ml)

3 tbsp rice wine vinegar (45ml)

2 tbsp sesame oil (30ml)

1 tbsp fresh ginger, grated (15ml)

3 garlic cloves, finely diced

Pinch of dried chili flakes (optional)

Splash of Tabasco sauce

Salt and pepper to taste

Directions:

- Combine ingredients in a small saucepan and bring to a simmer for 5 minutes.

- Let stand for at least an hour to mellow and blend.

Yield: 8 servings

Fish

Fennel Crusted Tuna

Whole Trout with Breadcrumbs & Anchovies

Trout with Prosciutto and Sage

Trout with Blackberry Glaze

Salmon with Strawberry Salsa

Grilled Haddock with a White Wine Garlic Sauce

Grilled Swordfish with Caribbean Salsa

Grilled Sea Bass with Mango & Red Onion Salsa

Grilled Grouper with Almond Butter

FENNEL CRUSTED TUNA

I'm begging you, please don't overcook the tuna. It should be served medium rare just like a nice lean cut of beef. Medium at best, okay? Otherwise it's just going to be dry and a waste of your time, money and taste buds. The classic coating for a tuna steak is crushed peppercorns. Using fennel seeds gives this dish a nice mellow licorice kick.

2 1-inch-thick tuna steaks (1 lb/450g each)

1 tbsp plus 1 tsp of crushed fennel seeds (20ml)

1 tbsp plus 2 tsp of minced lemon zest (25ml)

1 tsp kosher salt (5ml)

Olive oil spray

Lemon wedges

Directions:

- In a bowl, combine fennel seeds, lemon zest and salt and rub coarsely into flesh of the tuna. Cover tuna with plastic wrap and refrigerate for 2 hours.

- Remove the tuna from the fridge and let come to room temperature 30 minutes before grilling.

- Preheat the barbecue to high heat and oil the grill.

- Drizzle oil over tuna, season with salt and pepper.

- Place tuna on grill and cook for 2 minutes per side.

- Serve with fennel tops and lemon wedges as garnish

Serves 4

WHOLE TROUT WITH BREADCRUMBS AND ANCHOVIES

I love cooking whole trout. You get the added flavor bonus of cooking on the bone. For you fish-bone-adverse people out there, these bones peel away from the flesh quite easily. This is our play on a classic trout dish with breadcrumbs. The anchovies and rosemary make for an interesting taste combination. Serve this with couscous salad and some grilled carrots.

4 whole fresh trout, 3/4 lb each (340g)
    scaled and cleaned

5 tbsp extra virgin olive oil (75ml)

1 medium Spanish onion, minced

1 egg

3 tbsp chopped fresh parsley (45ml)

1 tbsp anchovy paste (15ml)

1 tsp fresh rosemary, minced (5ml)

2 tsp fresh thyme, (10ml)

1 1/2 cups coarse fresh white breadcrumbs
    (375ml)

Salt and pepper to taste

Toothpicks in water for one hour

Directions:

- Heat 3 tbsp (45ml) of oil in skillet over medium heat. Add onions and sauté until soft. Transfer to large bowl and cool.

- Add the egg and 2 tbsp (30ml) parsley, the anchovy paste, rosemary and thyme. Mix in breadcrumbs until well combined.

- Season the stuffing with pepper to taste.

- Season the fish cavities with salt and pepper

- Spoon stuffing into cavity (do not pack tightly). Use toothpicks to close cavity.

- Preheat barbecue to 375F/190C.

- Brush the grill with oil.

- Brush the trout all over with 1 tbsp (30ml) oil. Season the skin with salt.

- Place whole trout on the grill and cook for 5–7 minutes per side with the lid down.

- Using metal spatula, transfer fish to platter. Remove toothpicks and sprinkle fish with remaining parsley.

Serves 4

TROUT WITH PROSCIUTTO AND SAGE

Check out how easy this recipe is. The sage and prosciutto combo are perfect with the sweet juicy trout meat.

6 trout, 10 oz (315 g) each, cleaned, boned
    and scaled, with heads intact

Salt and pepper to taste

2 tsp freshly ground pepper (10ml)

24 fresh sage leaves

12 large thin slices of prosciutto

1/2 cup olive oil (125ml)

Directions:

- Prepare grill to medium heat

- Cut shallow diagonal slits in the meatiest part of both sides of the fish.

- Season both the inside and outside of the fish with salt and pepper.

- Place 4 sage leaves in the cavity of each fish.

- Place two slices of proscuitto down vertically so that they overlap slightly.

- Starting at end closest, place a fish perpendicular to the prosciutto and roll to cover fish.

- Brush both sides of the fish generously with olive oil and place gently on the grill.

- Turn only once during the cooking process when the prosciutto is nice and golden brown, about 4–5 minutes a side.

Serves 6

TROUT WITH BLACKBERRY GLAZE

You can have your friendly local fishmonger skin the trout for you if you'd like. While
we make lots of noise about using fresh ingredients, frozen berries are actually better
for the glaze because of their consistency. As always, the chipotle adds a smoky heat
to the dish. Serve a big red wine with lots of berry flavors like a Zinfandel or a Shiraz.

6 6oz trout fillets, skin removed (6 x 170 g)

2 tbsp olive oil (30ml)

Salt and pepper to taste

Blackberry Glaze

2 cups previously frozen blackberries,
    defrosted (500ml)

Juice of 1 lime

1 chipotle chili, seeded and diced

1 tbsp chopped fresh ginger (15ml)

1 tbsp sugar (15ml) or to taste

Salt and pepper to taste

Cilantro sprigs to garnish

Directions:

- Place defrosted blackberries in a colander set over a bowl. Allow the juice to drain through by pressing down with a spatula. You should have 1 cup (250ml) of juice in a bowl. Discard any seeds.

- In a small saucepan combine the limejuice, chipotle, ginger, sugar, salt and pepper. Add the reserved blackberry juice.

- Set over medium-high heat to simmer for 5 minutes. Strain into a bowl and set aside.

- Preheat barbecue to 375F/190C or medium-high heat.

- Drizzle trout fillets with oil and season with salt and pepper.

- Oil barbecue grill.

- Grill trout for 2 minutes or until golden char marks are achieved. Flip the trout and continue to cook for 3 minutes. Baste the trout continuously with the blackberry glaze. Remove trout from grill when desired doneness is achieved. Serve hot with remaining blackberry sauce and cilantro sprigs.

Serves 6

SALMON WITH STRAWBERRY SALSA

There's salmon and then there's *salmon*. Fresh before frozen. Wild before farmed.
Salmon is a great fish that doesn't need a lot of messing around when you cook it.
The strawberry salsa works really well if you serve a nice Viognier or fruity
Chardonnay.

1 center cut side of salmon, skin on

1 tbsp freshly ground pepper (15ml)

Juice of 1 lemon

Juice of 2 limes

2 tbsp chopped fresh thyme (30ml)

2 tbsp chopped oregano (30ml)

2 tbsp olive oil (15ml)

Salt and pepper to taste

Aluminum foil

1 tsp vegetable oil for brushing foil (5ml)

Strawberry Salsa

1 cup chopped strawberries (250ml)

1 tsp lime juice (5ml)

1 tsp balsamic vinegar (5ml)

1 tsp sugar (5ml)

1 tsp cracked black pepper (5ml)

1 tbsp chopped mint (15ml)

Directions:

- Cut the salmon into 6 pieces.

- Place the salmon in a non-reactive dish. Squeeze lemon and lime juice over the fish. Sprinkle with chopped herbs and drizzle with oil. Let sit for 30 minutes.

- Preheat the barbecue for indirect cooking at 325F/160C with one side turned off.

- Place the salmon on a sheet of aluminum foil that has been brushed with vegetable oil.

- Place the salmon on the side that's turned off, close the lid and cook for 20–25 minutes or until desired doneness.

- Remove from grill, place on platter and serve with strawberry salsa.

Serves 6

Strawberry Salsa Directions:

- Clean and hull the core from strawberries, chop into 1/4-inch dice and place in a medium bowl.

- In a separate small bowl whisk together lime juice, balsamic vinegar, sugar and black pepper until well combined.

- Pour over strawberries, sprinkle with freshly chopped mint and gently mix.

- Serve immediately. Don't let it sit too long or the berries will get mooshy.

Yield: 1 cup (250ml)

GRILLED HADDOCK WITH A WHITE WINE GARLIC SAUCE

Haddock is a fish most people don't think of right away. It's a saltwater fish related to cod and has a sweet mild taste. It's perfect for people who don't like fish that taste fishy. (Huh?) This simple sauce doesn't overpower the fish. Grilled asparagus goes really well with this one.

3 haddock fillets, cut in half

2 tbsp olive oil (30ml)

Salt and pepper to taste

White wine garlic sauce

1/4 cup diced shallots (62ml)

2 1/2 cups white wine (375ml)

2 cloves roasted garlic

3 tbsp cold butter, cut into cubes (45ml)

Directions:

- Preheat the barbecue to medium-high heat and oil the grill.

- Drizzle the fillets with oil and season with salt and pepper.

- Place the fish delicately on the grill and cook for 2 minutes per side.

- For the sauce, put the wine and shallots in a saucepan and reduce by half. Add roasted garlic and using a hand blender mix thoroughly.

- Bring the sauce to a gentle boil. Remove from heat; add the butter gradually and whisk to incorporate.

- Strain sauce and keep on low heat until ready to serve. Drizzle over haddock.

Serves 6

GRILLED SWORDFISH WITH CARIBBEAN SALSA

Swordfish is meaty and holds up well on the grill. Make sure the coconut is unsweetened and adjust the hot sauce to suit your tastes. Serve the swordfish with grilled sweet potato and a nice Riesling. Make extra and invite me over. I'll bring dessert.

Caribbean Salsa

1/3 cup red onion, minced (75ml)

3 oranges, peeled with pith removed, seeded, sectioned and halved

1 1/2 cups vine ripened tomatoes, chopped and seeded (350ml)

Directions:

- Prepare salsa by combining all ingredients; toss.

- Cover and refrigerate to set up for an hour before serving.

- In a bowl, combine oil, wine, thyme, garlic, and shallots.

1/3 cup fresh parsley, chopped (75ml)

1/3 cup fresh cilantro, chopped (75ml)

1/4 cup shredded fresh coconut
  (unsweetened) (60ml)

Juice of one lemon

Juice of one lime

Juice of one orange

3 tbsp balsamic vinegar (45ml)

Splash of hot sauce

6 swordfish steaks 6 oz. each, cut 1-inch thick

1/3 cup of extra virgin olive oil (75ml)

2/3 cup of white wine (150ml)

Thyme sprigs

3 cloves garlic, minced

3 shallots, minced

- Put the swordfish steaks in a large sealable plastic bag.

- Pour the marinade over the swordfish steaks and marinate for 20 minutes.

- Preheat grill to high heat.

- Remove the steaks from the marinade and pat dry with paper towels.

- Place the steaks on the grill and cook for approximately 4 minutes per side until opaque at the center.

- Serve with salsa on top.

Serves 6

GRILLED SEA BASS WITH MANGO AND RED ONION SALSA

There's been a lot of talk about sea bass being an endangered species. Chilean sea bass in particular has been almost fished out. Bass is sort of a generic catch-all name for lots of fresh and saltwater white fish that aren't even related. The best way to assuage extinction concerns is to find yourself a good fishmonger.

4 1/2 lb sea bass fillets (approx 2 kg)

4 tbsp olive oil (60ml)

Salsa

1 mango, chopped small

1 red bell pepper, chopped small

1 red onion, chopped small

1 fresh jalapeno pepper, chopped fine

1/4 cup cilantro, chopped (62ml)

1 tsp ground garlic (5ml)

1/4 cup pineapple juice (62ml)

6 tbsp fresh lime juice (90ml)

Salt and pepper, to taste

Spice Rub

1 tbsp dried basil (15ml)

1 tbsp dried thyme (15ml)

1 tbsp salt (15ml)

1 tbsp fresh cracked black pepper (15ml)

Directions:

- Mix all salsa ingredients together and set aside. Refrigerate until ready to use.

- Mix all spice rub ingredients together in a small bowl.

- Brush the fish fillets with olive oil and rub 1 tbsp of the spice rub into each fillet and let sit for 5 minutes.

- Preheat the barbecue to medium high.

- Grill the fish for 4 minutes per side.

- Serve with salsa.

Serves 4

GRILLED GROUPER WITH ALMOND BUTTER

Make sure your fishmonger removes the skin from your fillets. This is a nice juicy fish with a sort of delicate taste that works nicely with the almond extract in the butter. Go for a lighter wine like a pino gris or a sauvignon blanc with this dish.

4 grouper fillets

4 tbsp olive oil

Salt and pepper to taste

Almond Butter

1/2 cup (1 stick) unsalted butter, softened
(125ml)

4 oz almonds, crushed

2 tsp parsley, diced (10ml)

Splash of almond extract

Directions:

- Mix the butter, almonds, parsley and almond extract together in a bowl. Roll up into a log in plastic wrap and rest in the fridge for at least 1 hour.

- Preheat the grill to high heat. Season grouper with oil, salt and pepper and place onto oiled grill for 3 1/2 minutes per side.

- Remove from grill and serve warm with almond butter discs melting on top.

Serves 4

Seafood

Bucket of Clams with Lemon Grass Butter

Barbecued Peppered Mussels

Smoked Prosciutto-Wrapped Cheesy Shrimp

Grilled Shrimp in Peanut Sauce

Asian Grilled Shrimp

Grilled Oysters on the Shell

Grilled Octopus

Crab Burgers

Grilled Lobster Tail with Curried Butter

Grilled Scallops with Apple Cider Accent

Scallops with Parmesan Crust

BUCKET OF CLAMS WITH LEMON GRASS BUTTER

The name of this dish pretty much says it all. Like most things in life, size does matter when it comes to clams, only here you want smaller instead of bigger. Serve with lots of really good crusty bread.

1 lb fresh clams (450g)

Lemon Grass Butter

1/2 cup butter, melted (125ml)

2 cloves garlic, chopped

1 cup tomatoes, chopped (250ml)

Juice of 1 lemon

3 tbsp white wine (45ml)

1 tsp hot pepper flakes (5ml)

1 stalk lemon grass, peeled and chopped

Directions:

- Put all of the Lemon Grass Butter ingredients into a pot and let simmer over medium high heat until flavors are infused.

- Preheat grill to medium high.

- Scrub and rinse clams well.

- Place the clams on the grill with tongs, cook for 4 minutes or until all clams have opened. (Discard any that do not open.)

- Remove clams from grill, place in large bowl or bucket. Pour lemon grass butter mixture over top of clams. Serve immediately.

Serves 6

BARBECUED PEPPERED MUSSELS

If you've been reading through this book, you know how much I hate overcooking. It's a natural instinct to leave something on the heat for a minute or two or more when you're unsure. Mussels are sweet and juicy and dry out easily – they are ready to eat as soon as they open. Discard ones that don't.

2 1/4 lbs mussels, cleaned, sorted and
*   debearded (1 kg)*
1 cup of vermouth (250 ml)
Cold water to cover
2 bay leaves

Herbed Butter

1/2 cup room temperature butter 125 g
1 tbsp brined green peppercorns, drained,
*   coarsely chopped (15ml)*
1 tsp the brine from the peppercorns (5ml)
2 tbsp chopped fresh parsley (30ml)
1 tbsp chopped fresh tarragon (15ml)
1 tbsp chopped fresh thyme (15ml)
1 tbsp chopped fresh chives (15ml)
2 tsp freshly grated lemon zest (10ml)

Directions:

- Place cleaned mussels in a large stock pot and cover with the vermouth and water. Add bay leaves and bring to a boil. Steam for 4 minutes or until they are all open. Remove from the liquid.

- Meanwhile, prepare butter. Combine all of the butter ingredients and mix well.

- Remove and discard the top shell from each mussel.

- Spread herbed butter onto each mussel (overtop of meat) and place face-up on a perforated grill tray.

- Preheat the grill to medium high. Place the tray of mussels on the grill until heated through and the butter melts.

- Serve with lots of good bread, cheese and salad.

Serves 6

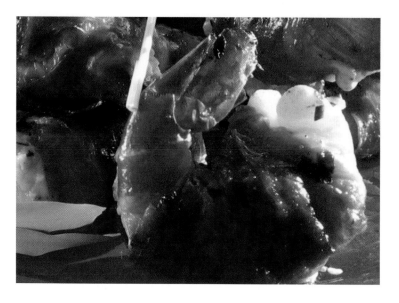

SMOKED PROSCIUTTO-WRAPPED CHEESY SHRIMP

This recipe calls for a dozen "6/8" shrimp. This means there will be 6 to 8 shrimp per pound. Ask your fishmonger to peel, devein and butterfly the shrimp for you. If he can't or won't do it, suggest he consider a career in real estate sales instead. You have *never* had shrimp like this: stuffed with cheese and wrapped in cured ham and grilled. This works well on a simple arugula salad.

12 6/8 shrimp, peeled, deveined and
  butterflied
1/2 cup cream cheese (125ml)
1/2 cup goat cheese (125ml)
2 tbsp chopped chives (30ml)
2 tbsp roasted garlic (30ml)
Salt and pepper to taste
12 sheets proscuitto, thinly sliced
1 tbsp olive oil (15ml)

Directions:

- In a medium bowl, mix cheeses, chives, roasted garlic and salt and pepper.

- Place about a tbsp of stuffing inside each shrimp, spread evenly.

- Fold the shrimp over and wrap with a strip of prosciutto, ensuring the stuffing is not exposed.

- Drizzle shrimp with oil.

- Preheat barbecue to medium heat.

- Place shrimp on a well oiled grill.

- Cook for 2–3 minutes per side or until prosciutto is crispy and shrimp is opaque.

- Remove form heat and serve immediately.

Serves 6

GRILLED SHRIMP IN PEANUT SAUCE

Shrimp has a pretty unique taste – it's not like you're going to mistake it for anything else. But it also absorbs whatever flavors you throw at it. Nice shrimp.

1 1/2 lbs of 6/8 shrimp, shelled and deveined

3/4 cup coconut milk (188 ml)

1/3 cup lime juice, freshly squeezed (84ml)

3 cloves garlic, minced

1 tsp salt (5ml)

1 tsp ground pepper (5ml)

Directions:

- Rinse the shrimp and pat dry with paper towel.

- Place in a large sealable plastic bag.

- In a bowl, combine the coconut milk, lime juice, garlic, and salt and pepper.

- Pour over the shrimp and marinate for 30 minutes at room temperature.

Sauce

3 tbsp extra virgin olive oil (45ml)

5 cloves garlic, minced

1 bunch scallions, green and white parts
    minced

2 tbsp fresh ginger, minced (30ml)

1/2 medium green pepper, stemmed,
    seeded and finely chopped

1/2 medium red pepper, stemmed, seeded
    and finely chopped

2 fresh tomatoes, peeled, seeded and
    finely chopped

1 1/4 cup coconut milk

1/2 cup creamy peanut butter

5 tbsp freshly squeezed lime juice

1/4 tsp cayenne pepper

1/2 cup cilantro, freshly chopped (125ml)

Salt and pepper

- Meanwhile, in a saucepan over medium heat, sweat off the garlic, scallions and ginger in oil.

- Add the green and red pepper and continue to cook for 5 minutes.

- Add the tomatoes and cook for another 2 minutes until some of the liquid has evaporated.

- Stir in coconut milk, peanut butter, lime juice, cayenne and half of the cilantro.

- Reduce the heat to low and continue to cook uncovered for approximately 10 minutes until the sauce beings to thicken.

- Adjust the seasoning and set aside until it is time to serve.

- Preheat the grill to high.

- Remove the shrimp and discard the marinade.

- Pat the shrimp dry with paper towel.

- Oil the grill and cook the shrimp for 2 minutes per side until pink.

- Brush them with some of the peanut sauce after the first flip.

- Sprinkle the remaining cilantro into the sauce just prior to serving.

Serves 8

ASIAN GRILLED SHRIMP

Chinese five-spice powder is a combination of cinnamon, cloves, fennel, star anise and peppercorns. Any decent grocery store will stock it or even better, experiment and make your own.

1 lb 6/8 shrimp, shelled and deveined (450g)

1 tsp sesame oil (5ml)

1 tbsp rice wine (15ml)

1 tbsp soy sauce (15ml)

1 tbsp honey (15ml)

1 tbsp sesame seeds (15ml)

2 tsp five-spice powder (10ml)

3 garlic cloves, whole, smashed

4 slices fresh ginger

Directions:

- Combine all of the ingredients in a sealable bag and mix well. Leave to marinate for 30 minutes.

- Preheat the grill to high heat.

- Oil the grill. Remove the shrimp from the marinade and place directly on the grill. Reserve the marinade.

- Cook for 2 minutes per side until pink.

- Put the remaining marinade in a saucepan and bring to a simmer. Reduce by half and drizzle over cooked shrimp.

Serves 4 as an appetizer

GRILLED OYSTERS ON THE SHELL

As a rule I think oysters should be eaten raw but this is a nice change now and then.

Crushed iced for serving

12 oysters

1 lemon, sliced into wedges for squeezing

Directions:

- Preheat the barbecue to medium high.

- Spread out crushed ice on a platter and keep it chilled while preparing the oysters.

- Make sure all oysters are tightly closed, and discard any that are not.

- Place the oysters directly on the grill, with the deep side down, so that when they open the juices will remain in the lower shell. Close the lid. The oyster will begin to open after 3–5 minutes.

- With oven mitts and a sharp knife or shucker, open oysters fully. Remove the oyster from the flat side of the shell and place them with the juices on the deep side of the oyster shell. Place on the ice bed.

- Discard any oyster shells that do not open. Sever with lemon wedges and enjoy!

Serves 2

GRILLED OCTOPUS

You are truly blessed if you live somewhere you can get fresh octopus. Frozen will have to do otherwise. This ain't no rubbery roadhouse calamari. Grilled octopus is a real treat.

2 lbs cleaned, trimmed octopus (900g)

2 tbsp fresh lemon juice (30ml)

3 tbsp red wine vinegar (45ml)

8 tbsp extra virgin olive oil (120ml)

1 tbsp dried oregano (15ml)

1 tsp coarse salt (5ml)

1 tsp cracked black pepper (5ml)

1/4 cup finely chopped parsley (62ml)

Directions:

- Preheat the barbecue to medium-high heat and oil the grill.

- Scrape any reddish skin off of the octopus.

- Leave the legs whole and cut the body into quarters.

- Rinse the octopus under cold water and blot dry.

- You can thread the legs onto long metal skewers or place them directly onto the grill.

- Arrange the octopus on the grill and turn every minute or so until they are nicely charred on all sides (about 3 minutes per side – 8–12 minutes in all).

- Cut the grilled octopus into bite sized pieces and place in a bowl.

- Mix remaining ingredients together. Pour over the octopus and toss. Leave the octopus to marinate for 30 minutes.

- Adjust seasoning and serve with lemon wedges.

Serves 4–6

CRAB BURGERS

Make sure you pick through the crab meat with your fingers to find any bits of shell that might be in there. This is a variation on the venerable crab cake. The breadcrumbs will brown up nicely on the grill and the jalapeno adds a bite to the mild crab.

6oz fresh crab meat (180g)

1 1/2 cups breadcrumbs (375ml)

1 cup finely chopped green onion (125ml)

1 tsp finely chopped jalapeño

2 1/2 tbsp mayo (37ml)

1/2 tsp celery salt (2.5ml)

1/2 tsp ground black pepper (2.5ml)

1 tbsp lemon zest

Juice of 1 lemon

1 egg

1 1/2 tbsp Dijon mustard (22ml)

Directions:

- Combine all of the ingredients – except 1/2 cup (125ml) of breadcrumbs – into a bowl and mix.

- Form into patties.

- Dip each patty into remaining breadcrumbs.

- Cover and refrigerate until time to grill. Remove from the fridge 15 minutes before grilling.

- Heat the barbecue to medium high and oil the grill.

- Grill the burgers for 5 minutes per side until golden brown.

- Serve on grilled onion buns with garlic aioli and sprouts

Serves 4

GRILLED LOBSTER TAIL WITH CURRIED BUTTER

It's pretty impossible to find fresh lobster tails, so go for frozen. The thing to do is find a decent fishmonger who turns over his or her inventory on a regular basis. You don't want to pay big bucks for a lobster tail that's been sitting in the freezer forever.

6 lobster tails (6–8oz each), previously
frozen, thawed and cleaned
Juice of 3 limes

Curried Butter

8 tbsp (1 stick) of unsalted butter at
room temperature (125ml)
1 tsp curry powder (15ml)
1/2 tsp dried thyme (2ml)
1/2 tsp cayenne powder (2ml)
1/2 tsp cumin (2ml)
1/2 tsp ground cardamom (2ml)
1/4 tsp salt (1ml)

Directions:

- In a large bowl mix all of the spices with the softened butter.

- Turn the lobsters upside down with the shell on the counter, and using kitchen shears cut along the inner shell to expose the meat.

- Pull the shell open to about an inch wide.

- Squeeze about 1/2 tbsp (7.5ml) of lime juice on each tail. Spread a tbsp of the curry butter over each tail.

- Preheat the grill to medium-low heat

- Place the lobster tails shell-side down on the grill and cook for approximately 10 minutes or until the meat is opaque.

Serves 6

GRILLED SCALLOPS WITH APPLE CIDER ACCENT

Scallops are meaty yet delicate in flavor. They dry out very quickly so please don't overcook. Make sure you pat them dry with paper towel before skewering.

24 large sea scallops

3 tbsp olive oil (45ml)

2 tsp salt (10ml)

1 1/2 tsp ground black pepper (7.5ml)

Juice of 2 lemons

1 cup apple cider (250ml)

8 wooden skewers soaked in cool water
    for 1 hour.

Directions:

- Place 3 scallops on each skewer and drizzle with olive oil, salt and pepper.

- In a small bowl, combine lemon juice and apple cider.

- Preheat barbecue to medium high and oil the grill with a lightly oiled cloth.

- Place scallops on grill (1–2 minutes per side) and baste continuously with lemon cider mixture.

Serves 8

SCALLOPS WITH PARMESAN CRUST

Crusty scallops on the barbecue? You bet. These guys are great on a little mixed green salad or as a side with a steak or a lobster tail.

1 1/2 lbs sea scallops (675g)

3 tbsp melted butter (45ml)

8 wooden skewers, soaked in water
  for an hour

Coating

1/2 cup finely crushed melba toast crumbs
  (125ml)

5 tbsp parmesan cheese, grated (45ml)

1 tbsp parsley, chopped (15ml)

Paprika to taste

Directions:

- In a sealable bag, combine all coating ingredients and shake well. Brush the scallops with melted butter and toss into baggie. Shake to coat well.

- Preheat the barbecue to medium high and oil the grill.

- Skewer the scallops through center of meat and place on the grill to cook for 2 minutes per side.

- Remove and serve immediately.

Serves 8

A

Almond Butter, 216
antipasto, grilled, 166
Apple Slaw, 28
applesauce
    passion fruit, 200
Apricot Mustard Glaze, 147
arugula
    avocado, grapefruit, red onion,
        and feta salad, 175
    corn and red pepper salad, 176
    salad, with pine nuts,
        cranberries, and dressing, 172
asparagus
    and beets, grilled, 167–68
avocado
    grapefruit, red onion, and feta
        salad, 175

B

baby back ribs. See Pork
back ribs. See Pork
bacon. See Pork
balsamic onion marmalade, 54
banana
    and potato salad, 180
    salsa, 196
barbecue sauces. See Sauces
barbecuing
    charcoal, 4–5
    cooking methods, 2–3
    equipment, 4, 8, 10
    gas, 4–5
    temperature assessment, 5
    tips, 6–10
Basting Butter
    for turkey, 35
beans, green
    salad, 183
beef
    brisket, 93–94
    filet mignon, 85–86
    hamburgers, 89–90
    hot dogs, 95
    kabobs, five-spice, 84
    prime rib, 82–83
    rib steak, 87–88
    sandwiches, 91–92
    short ribs, 79
    short ribs, Korean, 80–81
    tenderloin, 85–86
    top sirloin roast, 91–92
    veal chops, 98–99, 103
    veal loaf, 100

veal loin, and prosciutto, 105–6
veal loin roast, stuffed, 101-2
veal ribs, 107–8
veal roast, 104
veal shoulder, 96–97
beer marinade, 51
beets
    and asparagus, grilled, 167–68
black bean dipping sauce, 22
Blackberry Glaze, 208
Blackberry Pink Peppercorn
    Marinade, 117
brine for turkey, 34
Brown Ale Maple Glaze, 24
burgers. See Hamburgers; Lamb,
    burgers
butters
    almond, 216
    basting, for turkey, 35
    for clams, 218
    curried, 227
    garlic anchovy, 165
    for grouper, 216
    herbed, 90, 219
    lemon grass, 218
    for lobster tail, 227
    maple spiced, 163
    for mussels, 219
    Pernod, 200

C

cabbage
    coleslaw, Asian flavored, 171
    salad, 181
Caesar salad, 173
carrots
    grilled, 169
    marinated, 157–58
    salad, 182
cauliflower
    kabobs, 148–49
chicken
    breasts, smoked, marinated in
        port, 29–30
    breasts, stuffed, 19–20
    breasts in white wine tarragon
        sauce, 15–16
    breasts with herbs, 14
    brick, 12–13
    drumsticks, and bacon, 26
    legs, grilled lemonade, 17–18
    legs, spicy barbecued, 21
    teriyaki, 27
    thighs, Caribbean style, 25

thighs, with black bean sauce, 22
thighs and drumsticks, with
    coffee and pepper rub, 28
wings, brown ale and maple-
    glazed, 23–24
chicory
    chorizo salad, 174
chili
    hot, barbecue sauce, 193
chipotle-maple glaze, 160
chorizo
    chickory salad, 174
chutneys. See also Sauces
    Plum Chutney, 197
clams
    with lemon grass butter, 218
coleslaw
    Asian flavored, 171
cooking methods, 2–3
corn
    on the cob, smoked, 159
    grilled, 160, 185–86
    red pepper and arugula salad, 176
    and vegetables, 154–55
Cornish hens
    smoked raspberry, 45–46
couscous
    salad with grilled vegetables, 187
crab burgers, 226
Curried Butter, 227

D

dessert
    pears, roasted and stuffed,
        161–62
dips
    for grilled vegetables, 156
dressings
    for arugula salad, 172
    Asian, 171
    for cabbage salad, 181
    for Caesar salad, 173
    for carrot salad, 182
    for coleslaw, 171
    for fennel and orange salad, 177
    for wild rice pecan salad, 184
duck
    breasts, lemon grass smoked, 36
    breasts, marmalade, 39–40
    Peking-style, spit roasted, 41–42

E

espresso barbecue sauce, 56

F

fennel
grilled, 165
and orange salad, 177
and tuna, 203
fish
grouper, grilled, 216
haddock, grilled, 211
salmon, with strawberry salsa, 209–10
sea bass, grilled, 214–15
swordfish, with Caribbean salsa, 212–13
trout, with blackberry glaze, 207–8
trout, with breadcrumbs and anchovies, 204–5
trout, with prosciutto and sage, 206
tuna, fennel crusted, 203
fruit
banana and potato salad, 180
banana salsa, 196
passion fruit applesauce, 200
pears, roasted and stuffed, 161–62
pears, stuffed, 86
plum chutney, 197
watermelon salad, 188

G

game hens
rotisserie, 43–44
garlic, roasted, 20
Garlic Anchovy Butter, 165
Garlic Anchovy Dip, 156
glazes
apricot mustard, 147
blackberry, 208
brown ale maple, 24
chipotle-maple, 160
for grilled corn, 160
for pork burgers, 68
for trout, 208
grapefruit
avocado, red onion, and feta salad, 175
grill
oiling, 5
grouper
grilled, with almond butter, 216

H

haddock

grilled, with white wine garlic sauce, 211
hamburgers
beef, with homemade ketchup, 89–90
crab, 226
lamb, 113–14, 115
pork, maple mustard, 67–68
portobello cheeseburgers, 143
herbed butter, 90, 219
Hoisin Barbecue Sauce, 126
hors d'oeuvre
antipasto, 166
hot dogs, 95

I

Injection Liquid, 31

J

jalapeno
stuffed, 150–51
jerk mango marinade, 108
jerk rub, dry, 52

K

kabobs
beef, five-spice, 84
cauliflower, 148–49
lamb, 112
lamb and fig, 110–11
mushroom, 142
ketchup, homemade, 90, 190–91

L

lamb
burgers, 113–14
burgers, Asian spiced, 115
chops, 116–17
chops, onion water, 118
and fig kabobs, 110–11
kabobs, 110–11, 112
leg, grilled, 121
leg, stufffed, 119–20
loin with rosemary, 124
rack, marinated in port, 122–23
ribs, 128–29
shanks, 125–26
souvlaki, 127
lemon honey sauce, 198
lemonade chicken, grilled, 17–18
Lemon grass Butter, 218
lobster tail
grilled, with curried butter, 227

M

mango jerk marinade, 108
Mango Orange Sauce, 40
Maple Mango Barbecue Sauce, 194
Maple Spiced Butter, 163
marinades
for beef kabobs, five-spice, 84
beer, 51
blackberry pink peppercorn, 117
for chicken wings, 23
for Cornish hens, 45
for duck breasts, 39
jerk mango, 108
for Korean Beef Ribs, 81
for lamb, leg, 119, 121
for lamb chops, 117
for lamb kabobs, 111, 112
for lamb ribs, 129
for lamb souvlaki, 127
for mushroom kabobs, 142
for Peking-style duck, 41
for pork belly, 72
for pork loin, 60–61
port, 29
port, for rack of lamb, 123
for veal chops, 99, 103
for veal loin, 105
for veal ribs, 108
for veal roast, 104
for vegetables, 157–58
marinating
method, 6
marmalade
onion balsamic, 54
mint sauce, sweet and spicy, 199
Mushroom and Red Wine Sauce, 88
mushrooms
balsamic grilled, 141
kabobs, 142
portobello cheeseburgers, 143
mussels
barbecued peppered, 219

O

octopus, grilled, 225
onions
balsamic, marmelade, 54
grilled, with apricot mustard glaze, 147
marinated, 157–58
red, and avocado, grapefruit, and feta salad, 175
stuffed smoked, 144–45

wedges, grilled, and bacon, 146
orange
    and fennel salad, 177
oysters
    on the shell, 224

P

passion fruit
    applesauce, 200
pasta
    salad, with grilled corn and
    jalapenos, 185–86
peach
    smoky barbecue sauce, 49
peanut sauce, 222
pears
    roasted, stuffed, 161–62
    stuffed, 86
Pernod butter, 200
Pesto Cream Sauce, 104
Plum Chutney, 197
plum sauce, 115
pork
    baby back ribs, dry jerk, 52
    baby back ribs, spicy coconut, 57
    baby back ribs, strawberry and
    jalapeno, 58–59
    baby back ribs, with balsamic
    onion marmalade, 53–54
    baby back ribs and spare ribs,
    48–50
    back bacon, 65
    bacon, 66
    bacon and onion wedges, 146
    burgers, maple mustard, 67–68
    butt, slow roasted, 69–70
    Canadian bacon, 65
    chops, smoked, 64
    cured belly, 66
    ground, 67–68
    loin roast, stuffed, 60–61
    ribs and barbecue sauces, 48–50
    shoulder, 76–77
    smoked belly, 71–72
    smoked ribs with espresso sauce,
    55–56
    spare ribs, beer smoked, 51
    spare ribs and baby back ribs,
    48–50
    suckling pig, 73–75
    tenderloin, stuffed, 62–63
port marinades, 29, 123
Portobello Cheeseburgers, 143
potatoes

and banana salad, 180
    curried roast, 137–38
    grilled, with herbs, 139
    rosemary smoked, 140
    salad, 179
    skins, spicy grilled, 135–36
    twice-grilled, 133–34
poultry, 12–46. See also Chicken;
Cornish hens; Ducks; Game hens;
Turkey

R

red pepper
    corn and arugula salad, 176
ribs
    beef, 79, 80–81
    lamb, 128–29
    pork, 48–50, 51, 52, 53–54,
    55–56, 57, 58–50, 58–59
    veal, 107–8
rice
    wild, and pecan salad, 184
rice cakes, grilled, 152–53
roasted garlic, 20
Root Beer Barbecue Sauce, 75
rubs
    applying, 6
    for bacon, 66
    for beef brisket, 94
    for beef short ribs, 79
    Cajun, 92
    coffee and pepper, 28
    dry jerk, 52
    for duck breasts, 37
    for game hens, 43–44
    Hot Times, 31
    for lamb shanks, 126
    for pork butt, 70
    for prime rib roast, 82
    for ribs, 58
    for sea bass, 215
    for smoked ribs, 55
    southwestern, 97
    spice, 25, 215
    for suckling pig, 74
    for turkey, 31, 34, 36
    for veal tenderloin, 101

S

salads
    Apple Slaw, 28
    arugula, 172
    arugula, avocado, grapefruit, red
    onion and feta, 175

arugula, corn, and red pepper,
    176
    avocado, grapefruit, red onion,
    and feta, 175
    banana and potato, 180
    cabbage, 181
    Caesar, 173
    carrot, 182
    chicory chorizo, 174
    coleslaw, 171
    corn, red pepper and arugula,
    176
    couscous, with grilled vegetables,
    187
    fennel and orange, 177
    green bean, 183
    pasta, with grilled corn and
    jalapenos, 185–86
    potato, 179
    potato and banana, 180
    tomato and grilled bread, 178
    watermelon, 188
    wild rice pecan, 184
salmon
    with strawberry salsa, 209–10
salsa. See Sauces
sandwiches
    beef, with barbecue sauce, 91–92
sauces
    banana, 196
    barbecue, 49, 56, 64, 75, 92, 126,
    192, 193, 194, 201
    basting for pork loin, 61
    basting for ribs, 53
    basting for veal roast, 104
    black bean dipping, 22
    Caribbean salsa, 212–13
    espresso barbecue, 56
    golden mustard barbecue, 192
    for haddock, 211
    Hoisin barbecue, 126
    hot chili barbecue, 193
    ketchup, homemade, 90, 190–91
    lemon honey, with garlic, 198
    mango and red onion salsa, 215
    mango orange, 40
    maple mango barbecue, 194
    mint, sweet and spicy, 199
    mushroom and red wine, 88
    passion fruit applesauce, 200
    peanut, 222
    pesto cream, 104
    plum, 115
    plum chutney, 197

root beer, 75
for salmon, 210
for shrimp, 222
smoky peach, 49
southern barbecue, 64
strawberry and jalapeno, 59
strawberry salsa, 210
sweet and tangy, 50
teriyaki, homemade, 27
tomatillo salsa, 195
white wine garlic, 211
white wine tarragon sauce, 15–16
scallops
    grilled, with apple cider, 228
    with parmesan crust, 229
sea bass
    grilled, with mango and red onion salsa, 214–15
seafood. See also Fish
    clams, with lemon grass butter, 218
    crab burgers, 226
    lobster tail, with curried butter, 227
    mussels, barbecued peppered, 219
    octopus, grilled, 225
    oysters on the shell, 224
    scallops, grilled, 228
    scallops, with parmesan crust, 229
    shrimp, Asian grilled, 223
    shrimp, in peanut sauce, 221–22
    shrimp, wrapped in prosciutto, 220
shrimp
    Asian grilled, 223
    cheesy, wrapped in prosciutto, 220
    grilled, in peanut sauce, 221–22
smoke pouch, 5–6
    for smoked duck breasts, 38
smoking, 5–6, 8
souvlaki, lamb, 127
spare ribs. See Pork; Ribs
Spice Rub, 25
squash, acorn
    smoked, 163–64
strawberry and jalapeno sauce, 59
Strawberry Salsa, 210
stuffing
    for Cornish hens, 46
    for lamb, leg, 120
    for pork loin, 61

for pork tenderloin, 62
for potatoes, 134
for smoked onions, 145
for suckling pig, 74
for turkey, 35
for veal tenderloin, 102
sweet potatoes, mashed, 83
swordfish
    grilled, with Caribbean salsa, 212–13

T
teriyaki sauce, homemade, 27
Tomatillo Salsa, 195
tomato
    and grilled bread salad, 178
trout
    with blackberry glaze, 207–8
    with breadcrumbs and anchovies, 204–5
    with prosciutto and sage, 206
tuna
    fennel crusted, 203
turkey
    basting butter for, 35
    brined smoked, 33–35
    legs, hickory smoked, 36
    smoked spiced, 31–32
tzatziki topping, 114

V
veal. See Beef
vegetables. See also Salads
    asparagus and beets, grilled, 167–68
    beets and asparagus, grilled, 167–68
    carrots, grilled, 169
    carrots, marinated, 157–58
    cauliflower kabobs, 148–49
    corn, grilled, 160
    corn and vegetables, 154–55
    corn on the cob, 159
    fennel, grilled, 165
    grilled, 156
    grilled, and couscous salad, 187
    jalapeno, stuffed, 150–51
    marinated, 157–58
    mushroom cheeseburgers, 143
    mushroom kabobs, 142
    mushrooms, balsamic grilled, 141
    onion, marmalade, 54
    onion wedges, 146
    onions, grilled and glazed, 147

onions, marinated, 157–58
onions, stuffed smoked, 144–45
portobello cheeseburgers, 143
potato skins, 135–36
potatoes, curried roast, 137–38
potatoes, grilled with herbs, 139
potatoes, rosemary smoked, 140
potatoes, twice-grilled, 133–34
radish, marinated, 157–58
squash, acorn, 163–64
sweet potatoes, 83
zucchini, stuffed grilled, 131–32

W
watermelon
    salad, 188
White Wine Garlic Sauce, 211
White Wine Tarragon Sauce, 15–16

Z
zucchini
    stuffed, grilled, 131–32